FOCUS MANIFESTING

11 LAWS
of Manifestation to Master Your Mind and Attention

Stay Consistent and Attract Success in a Universe of Distractions

RYUU SHINOHARA

Omen Publishing

© Copyright Omen Publishing LLC 2023 - All rights reserved.

The content contained within this book may not be reproduced, duplicated or transmitted without direct written permission from the author or the publisher.

Under no circumstances will any blame or legal responsibility be held against the publisher, or author, for any damages, reparation, or monetary loss due to the information contained within this book, either directly or indirectly. You are responsible for your own choices, actions, and results.

Legal Notice:

This book is copyright protected. This book is only for personal use. You cannot amend, distribute, sell, use, quote or paraphrase the content within this book, or any part thereof, without the consent of the author or publisher.

Disclaimer Notice:

Please note the information contained within this document is for educational and entertainment purposes only. All effort has been executed to present accurate, up to date, and reliable, complete information. No warranties of any kind are declared or implied. Readers acknowledge that the author is not engaged in the rendering of legal, financial, medical or professional advice.

The content within this book has been derived from various sources. Please consult a licensed professional before attempting any techniques outlined in this book.

By reading this document, the reader agrees that under no circumstances is the author responsible for any losses, direct or indirect, which are incurred as a result of the use of the information contained within this document, including, but not limited to, errors, omissions, or inaccuracies.

HOW TO GET THE MOST OUT OF THIS BOOK

I see it all the time. People read LOA book after LOA book without ever taking action on any of the insights they've gained or concepts they've learned. The last thing I want is for you to read this book, forget everything you read, and continue to live as you've lived. You picked this book up for a reason: to manifest positive change. These additional resources will help you along this journey.

>> Scan the QR Code above to get your free bonuses <<

Free Bonus #1: Manifestor Masterlist

In this document, you'll discover the top 3 daily habits for manifesting a life beyond your wildest dreams. Includes a simple layout to track your progress and instructions to get started today.

Free Bonus #2: Intention Journal

Journaling doesn't need to take 10 minutes away from your morning routine. In fact, if you structure it right, you can get it done in under a minute. This intention journal focuses on the essential components that make this practice so powerful.

Free Bonus #3: 4 Subtle Meditation Mistakes to Avoid

A deep meditative state can be challenging to come by. The mind and body will do everything possible to stop you from fully surrendering. If you truly want to maximize the benefits of your meditation practice, check out this document to avoid making the same mistakes millions are making.

Free Bonus #4: Meditation Design

There are many different ways to meditate. After testing many other methods, I've put together a step-by-step structure that I've found to be the most effective for deepening your state and embodying the future you.

Free Bonus #5: 4-Step Conscious Business Acceleration

Being an entrepreneur and business owner comes with many unique challenges and struggles. In this document, I'll provide you with an action plan for taking quantum leaps in your financial and business ventures.

Free Bonus #6: Vision Calendar

Are you struggling with consistency and clarity? The Vision Calendar is tailored to outline your daily/monthly/quarterly/yearly goals and intentions into bite-size pieces to prevent overwhelm and confusion.

Free Bonus #7: 4 Anti-Manifestation Practices

Sometimes people make mistakes. That's okay. Other times, they unconsciously sabotage themselves without even knowing it. This document will outline commonly taught manifestation practices that work against you and how to shift them to your benefit.

Scan the QR Code below to get your free bonuses:

CONTENTS

Introduction	7
Chapter 1: The Singularity of Goal Setting	14
Law #1	
Chapter 2: Presence Development	30
Law #2:	
Chapter 3: The Architect of Perception	44
Law #3	
Chapter 4: Spaces of Reality	59
Law #4	
Chapter 5: Social Synergy	74
Law #5	

Focused Manifesting

Chapter 6: Thought Prioritization   94

    Law #6

Chapter 7: Emotional Distractions   109

    Law #7

Chapter 8: Mental Stories of Self   122

    Law #8

Chapter 9: Narrowing Attention   137

    Law #9

Chapter 10: Realigning Your Focus   155

    Law #10

Chapter 11: Honing In   170

    Law #11

A Short Message From The Author   183

Bibliography   184

INTRODUCTION

When I first learned about manifestation, I was committed—although not in the way I'm going to be teaching you in this book. I was committed to the magic. The mystery. The unexpected. The surprise. The gifts, blessings, and successes I was not expecting. As a result, my manifestations were good, but random. This made them unpredictable, inconsistent, and *unsustainable*. For example, when I started my journey into entrepreneurship, I didn't know what type of business I wanted to get into. *What did I want to sell? Whom did I want to serve? What did I want to create?* I knew two things:

1. I wanted the freedom to travel and live life on my terms. I dreaded having to fit my life into someone else's schedule. (Goal #1)

2. I wanted to work on projects I'm passionate about (I didn't want to be the next toilet-paper-selling millionaire). (Goal #2)

I spent weeks watching tutorials, reading books, and listening to podcasts about successful people in all kinds of fields and spaces. I knew that whatever path I chose, I would commit my time, energy, and attention to it wholeheartedly. It was easy. The first business I jumped into (book publishing) gave me the two things listed above. The reasons? I had space to think for myself. I had minor distractions and no social pressure from friends or family. Life was quiet. The only thing I could hear was the voice of my intuition. Taking this path was my choice alone—and that was the most exciting part. I wasn't confused. I didn't doubt myself. I was a irrational optimist. The moment I found out that I could create my own online business, travel the world, and make a living doing what I love, a switch flipped inside me. It felt like I was already walking the path of becoming a self-sovereign individual instead of following the traditional route I'd been on.

To many people's surprise, during the first two months of my journey, I studied the Law of Attraction and wrote *The Magic of Manifesting*—nine months later, it became an Amazon best-seller. However, the road got bumpy when I had to *stick to it*. I lacked genuine commitment, and my book didn't start making an impact until about a year later.

Within two months of publishing my book, I was bored. I felt like I needed a "killer opportunity" or a "secret" to get me to my desired reality. I was on the path to success, but distractions, shiny objects, and the promise of greener grass derailed me. I had published a book with potential, but quickly abandoned it. As a result, it disappeared into the abyss along with millions of other books. I looked around for opportunities without realizing the best one staring me in the face the entire time. Without hesitation, I scattered my energy across multiple goals and business ideas. When I realized this mistake, I had a breakthrough.

Before my breakthrough, I had been jumping around with a sporadic optimism that did nothing but keep my energy diluted. I realized, *Ryuu, you've got the right mindset, but you have to focus.*

So, I focused on writing meditation scripts and recording audios—publishing them on platforms like Audible and YouTube. Then I tried building an advertising agency for chiropractors—a money-focused endeavor. Cash ran low, and I got desperate—I needed a quick win. After a few weeks, I tried social media marketing for health professionals. In between these ideas, I invested time and money taking mentorship programs and building cryptocurrency portfolios, hoping and wishing one would give me the "secret answers" and "overnight success" I was seeking. Within four months, I was upwards of $7,000 in debt.

After many failures, losses, and struggles, it was the 2020 New Year. As I was journaling and reflecting on the previous six months, I realized that if I wanted my manifestations to be consistent and sustainable, I needed to build a solid foundation. I needed to choose a path I enjoyed, and to which I could commit at least twelve months. Sure, it's exciting to think that success can happen overnight or that your goal should be to manifest a $10,000 check magically. It's just not the best way to go about it. If this is how you manifest, you have to depend on random success after random success all the time. Then, the moment you're "off-frequency," you stop attracting the successes, and you get frustrated because it feels like your luck has run out. But that's life. It comes in waves. Ups and downs. This will never change. However, what can change is the general direction your life goes. When you build a solid foundation for your dream to grow, you don't need luck.

The laws I'm going to introduce to you in each chapter of this book are not just about helping you get into the frequency of your desires, but about helping you *stay in it* so you can attract more success as health, wealth, love, and happiness *consistently*. Imagine manifesting a random check for $10,000 but going back to living paycheck to paycheck a few months later. I don't want that. You don't want that. Nobody wants to attract a life they know is fleeting. It's like going on vacation, then spending the last few days thinking about what you're going to do when you go home.

What if every day can feel vacation-like? What if every day can feel like the manifestation of your dream? Struggles, obstacles, and challenges will still show up, but you'll experience them in a different reality, with a new set of beliefs and goals. When I struggle to write content for my emails or make a profit from investments, I'm doing it from a villa in Costa Rica after spending my morning on the beach. The dream isn't at risk because the foundation is there. From this position, the challenge becomes to sustain, live out, and grow the success you've already manifested—versus chasing the off chance you'll experience it again.

Everybody has desires. But few people understand that in order to manifest what you desire, you need to have a solid, high, sound structure to stand on. This is how you attract results and outcomes that stick to you like glue. This is the type of success that stays and becomes a part of your existence and identity. In order for this to happen, you need to master the skill of what I like to call *Focused Manifesting*.

What Is Focused Manifesting?

Where attention goes, energy flows. If you've read any book on the Law of Attraction, you're familiar with this statement. While authors and creators of hundreds of thousands of books, videos, courses, workshops, seminars, and retreats have repeated it, few people can apply it with mastery. They might find a bit of success, but it disappears as fast as it appeared. Why? Because their attention shifts. They redirect it to another goal or another exciting endeavor. The modern term for this is *Shiny Object Syndrome*, the act of chasing novelties, new highs, and possibilities. When we chase shiny things, we realize that what we set out to manifest does not come as quickly as we'd hoped. So, we jump on the next opportunity or the next idea, thinking, *this will be the one*. Some people spend years trying to find "the one," not realizing that had they committed to one path, they would already be where they want to be. They would have acquired the money, time, and freedom to live the life they've always desired.

Unfortunately, because we live in a consumer society, that's not how most people operate. Every single product or idea out there has the sole purpose of stealing your attention. Look around you. Notice the color and design of your coffee mug. The labels on your food packaging. The posters on your wall. The car in your driveway. It's all been designed meticulously to attract your attention, and to make you think, "I want this." It doesn't matter if it's good for you or not. That's not the point. The point is for you to buy it, use it, and give it your attention and energy. That's it. To believe someone created it to do anything else is to live disconnected from the reality of marketing that surrounds us and influences our decision-making daily. Not only does the external world distract us, it conditions us to distract ourselves—through our thoughts, urges, and cravings.

So, the purpose of this book is to curate your attention to be in alignment with the goals and aspirations you have for your life. We will do this by tackling four different aspects of your reality: your physical, mental, emotional, and spiritual spaces. We will show you how to not just be the receiver of blessings and successes, but to be the conscious creator of them. There are two forms of manifesting:

Focused Manifesting

1) Receiving: As a receiver, you depend on the Universe to give you what you want without establishing a clear structure or intention for acquiring it. For example, maybe you want to manifest a random check in the mail (without working for it) or maybe you want to attract more clients (without increasing expenses). Believing with all your heart in these events that have no clear and obvious cause (or evidence and proof they will happen) is like trying to convince yourself that your skin is blue—it's not an easy feat.

2) Creating: Some people use Universal Laws to their advantage—they are creators. They do this by optimizing their four spaces to develop clarity, evidence, and a conviction that they are becoming who they want to be and are attracting the things they want. When you are in the creator role, you build consistency with your manifesting practice, making everything you attract *stay for good*. Since you're focused on building from the ground up, you create a structure in your life that feeds your dream (versus depending on the Universe to do the heavy lifting).

Now there's a time and place for both receiving and creating. Working hard is necessary, but so is letting go, putting in the right amount of intention, and surrendering to a higher power. It's about knowing how to live in harmony with these two forces, and knowing which strategy to choose and when. That wisdom comes through practice. In this book, I'll show you how to refine your focus to meet the Universe halfway, so your manifestations go from being random, unexpected events to being predictable, sustainable, and effortless.

Who Is This Book For?

If you have found success with the Law of Attraction, but find it inconsistent, this book is for you. If you are tired of depending on random blessings or off-chance opportunities to keep your dream life alive, you'll find wisdom in this book that can turn things around. If you are living in anxiety about when your next manifestation is going to come save you, you are holding the solution to your dilemma in your hands. This book is about turning your entire life into a manifestation. It will show you how to live the dream while working to build and grow it.

My intention in writing this book is to help you find focus in a Universe riddled with distractions. The concepts we'll cover will help you focus your scattered mind, streamline your manifestation processes, and achieve exponential growth in your journey.

CHAPTER 1

THE SINGULARITY OF GOAL SETTING

Law #1: Follow the Soul

"Only the soul can know the algorithm of one's individual success."

Vadim Zeland

Ryuu Shinohara

There once was a man named Ethan who lived in a world filled with illusions and confusion. Like many others, it was easy for Ethan to get lost and feel desperate in this world. Shiny objects of all kinds were scattered about, placed in obscure, unexpected locations. People of all ages chased after these illusory prizes, believing they held the key to fulfillment and happiness. Ethan, a dreamer at heart, found himself stuck in this never-ending pursuit. He raced toward each glimmering object, convinced it held the answers he sought. But time and time again, his efforts were in vain. The shiny objects dissolved into thin air, leaving him with nothing but a hollow ache in his soul.

Day after day, Ethan sat, waited, and yearned for a better life, hoping that the next shiny object would bring him happiness. But the harder he chased his dreams, the more elusive they became. It seemed the world had conspired against him, feeding him illusions that drained his vitality and left him disheartened. Then, one fateful night, a faint twinkle of light pierced through Ethan's window, raising him from his slumber. A soft glow bathed his room, and an indescribable warmth enveloped his being. In that moment, he felt complete, as if he needed nothing else. It was a feeling he had longed for but had never experienced.

Enchanted by this newfound sensation, Ethan set out to uncover its origin. Instead of chasing after shiny illusions, he searched for that radiant light in every aspect of his life. Days turned into weeks, and weeks into months as he ventured through new, uncharted territories, both external and within himself.

Years passed, and as Ethan's journey unfolded, he understood the true nature of the light. It was not an external force or a shiny object to be grasped. Rather, it was a reflection, a glimmer that emanated from his heart. The sparkle he had sought had always been within him, waiting for him to recognize it. With this profound realization, Ethan's perspective shifted. He no longer chased after illusions, for he had discovered his source of joy and fulfillment. The light within his heart became his guiding star, illuminating his path as he navigated life's twists and turns.

And so, the man whom the chase had once consumed, who had been driven by illusions and temporary pleasures, now embraced his own genius. He cultivated the light within him, nurturing it with love, compassion, and self-acceptance. Ethan's pursuit of meaning and purpose transformed into a journey of self-discovery, and the radiance of his heart guided him to a life filled with peace, contentment, and genuine happiness.

The light of one's heart...our CHIEF AIM!

Defining Your Chief Aim

Manifestation concepts are easy to understand in a literary context, and that's why I came up with the "Story of Ethan." Like Ethan, a man lost in a world of illusions and distractions, many people go through life chasing after every shiny new object that promises to give them that "overnight success" they need in order to be happy or fulfilled. Often, these shiny things promise manifestations without you having to invest time, effort, and/or energy. At other times, they promise that if you give them all your time, effort, and energy, you are certain to manifest your desires. "*I hustle eighty hours a week…twice the average Joe!*" a man like Ethan would have boasted with a swollen chest, showing everyone that in the world of hustle, he stood above the rest.

While hard work is respectable (especially when engaging in a task you don't like doing), it also reveals that there is a *lack of flow* in relation to the manifesting process. If you're struggling to achieve your goals, it might be because you're chasing an *illusionary object of success*. You might get a cheap spike in satisfaction now and then, but the work isn't in alignment with your true nature. If you continue on this path mindlessly you might accumulate successes, but find yourself imprisoned in a state of perpetual work. Within personal development literature, authors mention that you need to "step into the unknown" or "do what's uncomfortable", and the Universe will respond. This is true. However, getting out there without a focus is counter-productive. While the Universe does work in mysterious ways beyond our human comprehension, there are certain *guiding principles* that allow us to move in accordance with these ways and which will help us align with the objectives our higher selves have designed for us.

Soul Goals, or purpose-driven objectives, are not shiny objects, they are guiding lights. Soul Goals go beyond simple desire and align with the intangible elements we seek to develop, build, and incorporate into our lives. For example, if someone is looking for a partner, they are looking for love, belonging, and family, etc. If someone is looking for money, they are looking for stability, freedom, and security.

Your genuine desire sits in the shadow of a shiny object. The shiny object keeps you occupied, entranced in a dynamic of stagnation and inconsistency. Since our world is flooded with shiny objects, it can seem like every path is a worthy path, when in reality, none of them are. *You* make the path worthy.

In my previous books, I talked about getting clear on your desires, so I will not go into detail about how to achieve that clarity. Instead, this section will help you *find your focus*. This starts by not just defining your desires, but by defining what aspects of reality align with your true nature (like your current beliefs, interests, and strengths). The human mind and heart are two sides of the same coin. Both intend the best for you, but in different ways. It's your job to put them both on the same page, creating what's known as *heart-mind synchronicity.*

There are many ways of achieving this: meditation, visualization, hypnosis, NLP, etc. However, it all starts with clarity around what you're being called to create. What attracts your heart (anticipation) and mind (believability)? What are you excited about manifesting? What do you believe you can manifest? That's the "sweet spot," as some would say. It all comes down to *clarity.* Once you get clear on what both your heart and mind want, you have identified your Chief Aim. Another way to look at this is by asking yourself: "What is that *one goal* that will lead to me fulfilling all my goals and desires? What is the *one task* that will facilitate everything else?"

In the book, *The ONE Thing: The Surprisingly Simple Truth About Extraordinary Results,* authors Gary Keller and Jay Papasan discuss this simple fact. They explain that by focusing on one goal, one that will provide the most return on investment in relation to your overall aim, everything else falls into place.

> "Make sure every day you do what matters most. When you know what matters most, everything makes sense. When you don't know what matters most, anything makes sense."

> Gary Keller

But how do we know what matters most? We listen to our soul. We listen to what our heart wants and what our mind needs. From there, we define our *one thing*, build a plan around achieving it, and pursue it. And, like Ethan after his epiphany, we ignore all the shiny objects along our path.

But here's a cold, shocking truth most books on manifestations do not mention. You *can* have it all, but not by trying. What do I mean by this? Well, every desire you've ever had is possible for you, but not if you're giving attention to all of them at the same time. Reality works in waves, not in big splashes. It comes in temporary seasons. You say "Yes" to one opportunity and say "No" to all others. You cannot be a "people pleaser" to your goals. That will drain you and keep you stuck in the chase. Instead, prioritize them. Create a hierarchy. By doing this, not only do you make more progress, but the goals you said "No" to become easier to achieve in the future. Sometimes, they achieve themselves, with no direct effort on your part.

Like a relay race, one goal should hand the baton (your attention) to the next, then the next, and so on. You can cover a larger distance when your goals feed themselves (versus you trying to feed them your attention all at once). Achieving your goals will happen naturally when you work in harmony with your heart and mind.

The Hierarchy of Goals

Your current beliefs and actions sustain your current reality. It would be foolish (and unwise) to abandon or neglect these elements right off the bat. Say, for example, you want to write a best-selling book, yet you're working nine to five. Your job is paying all of your bills and putting food on the table. Most people aren't willing to lock themselves in a cabin in the middle of the woods for three months, mainlining black coffee as they write their bestseller. It's unreasonable (and unnecessary) to put this kind of pressure on yourself.

Focused Manifesting

Those cards are not in your hand (yet). By that I mean you can't expect to find the *perfect time* or the *perfect place* to sit down to write your book. You need to adapt your Chief Aim to fit into your life without burning yourself out. That's no easy feat, right? Fortunately, you're reading this book. Throughout the rest of this section, we'll address this issue while still being true to Law #1: *Follow Your Soul.*

If you know what your Chief Aim is, it's your responsibility to incorporate it into your current reality. You can't always expect reality to change to accommodate you. Does this seem contradictory to what you're used to hearing? Were you taught to sit and wait for inspiration to come? Or wait until the Universe creates time and space for you to put energy into your new project? You could take that route, and it could work, but this is not how *true* creators direct their intentions. Creators don't wait. They create.

"But Ryuu," you ask, "How do I do this?"

First, you'll need to define your Chief Aim. Once you have defined it, you have to map out the actions required to make it happen. We'll discuss more of this in Chapter 2, but for now, let's move onto the next layer: *Maintenance Goals.* These are tasks you can't eliminate, or they'll dismantle the hierarchy. For example, doing your job, paying your bills, taking care of your kids, taking care of your health, etc. While these activities may take up the bulk of your time, they don't move you toward your Chief Aim. All they do is keep the boat afloat. By defining maintenance goals, you're auditing where your energy is required to keep the structure strong. (Note: Going to the bar with your buddies to watch the game is not a maintenance goal.)

You'll be surprised to see how many of your apparent "essentials" are, in fact, not essential. Chasing illusionary objects entangles you in actions you think are crucial, when really, they just sap you of energy and keep you locked in your current (less than ideal) reality. When you get clear on your maintenance goals, you know which actions to take care of first, second, third, etc. Once you have your Chief Aim and maintenance goals mapped out, it's time to reorganize your daily planner and to-do list.

Ideally, eighty percent of your energy should go to your Chief Aim, and the other twenty percent to your maintenance tasks. However, if you're working long hours and have obligations, eighty percent will most likely go into maintenance, while you spend the other twenty percent building. If you want to reach the next stage of the journey, over time, you'll need to hand over the baton. We'll discuss more about how to do this in a later chapter.

Of course, we could be sophisticated and create deadlines, schedules, and trackers, but the most important component is that you prioritize the *one thing*. All your other goals, like, "I want to learn Spanish," or "I want to take up surfing," and so on, are secondary, *back burner goals*. Let the Universe carry them out in the background, and let them unfold on their own. When you achieve your Chief Aim, you will have the resources, time, and energy to pursue your back burner goals. Therefore, none of them should take your attention or energy at this point. Focus on only those things that, once achieved, will get you closest to your end-goal.

For example, in my journey, I knew I wanted to travel the world, stay in exotic Airbnb's, immerse myself in new cultures, meet new people, and live a life defined by freedom. However, I was a broke university student, living with my parents, with $50.00 to my name. I needed a business. But not just any business. I needed one that gave me enough money, but also gave me time. My goal was never to get filthy rich. It was to become free. Free from having to work eight hours a day, Monday to Friday. Free from having to wake up at a specific time every morning. Free from having to stay in one city because of work. Free from being stuck in a routine that didn't feel like mine. This is when I set out to create content for the internet. This was my Chief Aim. Everything else (including my studies and job) was a maintenance goal. I couldn't ditch school or my parents would have had a fit. I couldn't ditch my job or I'd have no money to pay bills or invest in my business. I needed to keep these areas running to maintain harmony. Around eighty percent of my time was going into school and work, but that didn't stop me. Within twelve months of starting, my business had already replaced my job. During the early stages of my journey, I learned I didn't need time to build my dream. I needed to pay it attention.

Your Only Tool of Creation

As I said earlier, we live in a world similar to that of our fictional protagonist, Ethan—a world filled with distractions and shiny objects. Every little thing is screaming for our attention. This is not a coincidence. This is by design. The advertising industry spends hundreds of billions of dollars each year trying to capture your attention. While they might not say, "*Where your attention flows, energy goes…,*" they understand the principle. They know that if they have your attention, potentially, they have your money. They can inspire you to act on their offers, promotions, and ideas. While this is capitalistic, the Law of Attraction does not discriminate. If you understand the power of your attention and how to manage it, you will be able to co-create a reality beyond your wildest imagination. Because *your attention is your only tool of creation.*

The only real control you have over your life is how you manage your attention and what you focus on. Everything else is secondary. The thoughts you think, the emotions you feel, the time you have, and the actions you take—all are echoes of your focus.

Many people blame 'time' for why they're not where they want to be. The truth is, time is an illusion. You can spend two hours in front of your computer and get no work done, just like you can spend two hours at the gym and not lift a single weight. Time is irrelevant. The work you do within that time frame is also irrelevant. Why? Well, you can spend two hours in front of the computer, do a lot of work, and have nothing to show for it after four weeks, just like you can spend two hours every day at the gym lifting weights, and still make no progress. It's not about the work you do. It's about *where you place your attention within that work*.

When you focus your energy on the tasks that move you closer to your end goal, you can spend two hours in front of the computer daily, do a lot of work, and finish writing a book in four weeks, just as you can spend two hours at the gym every day, lift weights, and gain seven pounds of muscle mass in three months. Focused attention is the source of change and transformation.

The process of Focused Manifesting starts by defining your Chief Aim. Most people set too many goals, spread themselves thin, and end up giving little energy to each goal, making their progress slow and inconsistent. Learning to optimize your attention speeds up your path to growth and manifestation. When you understand what the *one goal* you should focus on is, the right thoughts and actions come. If you don't have a clue about what to prioritize, you'll be distracted, and your attention (your only tool of creation) will be in the hands of those multi-billion-dollar industries that are vying for your hard-earned dollars.

Leveraging Your State

Have you ever noticed that most Law of Attraction books talk about the concept of "co-creation?" You and the Universe coming together to create the life of your dreams? Many people would interpret this as "you need to take action" or "you need to meet the Universe halfway." This is a part of it, but there is another layer, and many people miss out on it.

We cannot measure all our desires in the same way. Not all desires carry the same level of *probability*. Some desires are long term, others are only for the next three months. It's possible to accomplish them all, but there is a timing you should respect. When deciding what your next goal should be, consider your current state, and then *leverage your state to decide which desires are worth prioritizing*. You do this, first, by defining the desires that are most exciting to pursue and most believable to achieve. Then, you prioritize them. However, we need to recognize the volatile nature of this approach.

Reality operates in waves. Therefore, not every desire you have will be exciting at every moment in your journey. There are desires you're curious about, that are urgent, or that are a necessary steppingstone before you can take your next step. There are desires you've been thinking about for five years and those you developed as you have been reading this book. Desires carry differing weights at different periods in your life. It's important to know this because once you recognize how your desires fluctuate, you're better able to adapt, define, and achieve your Chief Aim. For example, sometimes in my life, business needed to become a priority. Sometimes I prioritized travel and adventure. During different periods, my heart and mind aligned with different goals. Here's the strange part—this volatility is out of our conscious control.

The Universe, our intuition, and our soul all have unique plans for where we should focus. There's a famous Law of Attraction technique called "Follow the Breadcrumb Trail." It's the idea that you should follow your highest excitement and joy. Stop for a moment and check in with yourself. What area of your life feels the most expansive? Where do you feel you'll experience the most growth? Where would you learn the most lessons? Intuitively, what do you feel needs more of your attention? By recognizing these subtle impulses and inclinations, you're better able to discover the areas that you should prioritize, instead of falling victim to the ego and ideas imposed by society. Consider the timing and context of your current state and reality.

As we've discussed before, there are two ways you can measure your goals: *level of anticipation* and *level of believability.*

1. The first has to do with how excited you are about manifesting what it is you desire. If it's the most exciting thing in your list of goals and dreams, then it should be high on your list when deciding what your Chief Aim should be.

2. The second way to measure a goal is to assess your level of belief that you'll be able to accomplish it. It's common practice in the personal development space to multiply your goals tenfold. While I agree this can create a sense of excitement mixed with urgency, for many people, it can also be another reason to feel overwhelmed. It spreads your attention thin because you start to think about all the steps you need to take to get you there. By all means, set big, extravagant goals, but do not make those your primary focus. Prioritize goals that are believable, and just beyond your reach.

Therefore, to define your Chief Aim, pick a desire that's both exciting AND believable. Choose a goal that leverages both your heart's passion and your mind's rationale. When you do this, it's easier to "follow the breadcrumb trail" and stay consistent.

In the next chapter, we'll *deepen your sense of presence* and discuss how you can use it to maintain your focus and build momentum to accomplish your bigger, long-term goals.

CHAPTER 1 EXERCISES

Defining Goals

Write down all of the goals you have for the next year?

Anticipation Score

From 1-10, rate each goal with the level of anticipation you have for its achievement. How excited are you about it?

Believability Score

From 1-10, rate each goal with the level of believability you have for its achievement. How much do you believe you can achieve it?

Defining Chief Aim

Write down all of the goals that ranked the highest, then pick one to define as your Chief Aim.

Defining Maintenance and Back-Burner Goals

a) Write down a list of goals you need to maintain.

b) Write down a list of goals you need to put in the back-burner.

CHAPTER 2

PRESENCE DEVELOPMENT

Law #2:
The Present Moment
Is the Only Moment

"Desire is a contract that you make with yourself to be unhappy until you get what you want."

Naval Ravikant

"If only" are some of the saddest words in the Universe. How many people wait for an outcome or manifestation that never comes, thinking it will change their lives? Unfortunately, our society trains us to look at "final events" as the objects of our desire. You know, "Selling the millionth book," or "Getting that promotion," or "Bumping into Mr. (or Ms.) Right."

How many times a day do you daydream about the magical moments your life lacks? If you're like most people, you think about it all the time. I still do, too. Every time I experience the valleys of life, it reminds me of the peaks.

Under the "If only" premise, most people would let go of all responsibility for their situation and place it on the Universe. They would wait for a magical moment to appear. A knock on their door. An email in their inbox. A call on their phone. This is the mind's way of coming to terms with the invisible. Of accepting total defeat. It's comfortable and safe, and it prevents shattered expectations.

The mind is exceptional at coming up with excuses and stories of defeat, but the soul understands the truth. So, "If only" is sad because it severs any chance an individual has at manifesting their desired reality. Instead of saying "If only," replace these words with "What if?" or "Imagine...." This way, you include yourself in the future you're talking about, speaking it into existence.

We live under the illusion that once we reach a specific goal in life, we'll be happy, fulfilled, and loved. However, more often than not, we reach this destination only to find it empty. That feeling of accomplishment you're after? It doesn't last long. When our goals are outcomes, we put our joy and success on hold.

Focusing on outcomes leads you to chasing shiny objects. This path keeps you stuck in one way of being, or at one frequency, waiting

Focused Manifesting

until your physical reality changes. If you've read my previous books on the Law of Attraction, you'll know that the internal must change before the external follows suit. Your world reflects you.

Those shiny objects promise you the world. They appeal to your ego—the part of you that wants more material success to boast to the rest of your tribe. The ego is here to protect and secure your identity in the external world. Any threat to the ego—like stepping into discomfort, changing your patterns, or doing something you normally wouldn't do—will cause it to play all sorts of mind games and create narratives that keep you stuck in the familiar, even if the familiar is detrimental to you. When you can look past the ego, follow your heart, and live by the laws that govern the Universe, you can take massive strides toward your dream reality.

Now there's nothing wrong with wanting material success. It's fun to play the game of possessions. As I'm writing this, I'm in Los Angeles, California, the most material-success-driven city in the world. I see a Lamborghini, Porsche, or Ferrari every time I leave the house. Last week, I went to the Balenciaga store on Rodeo Drive and bought a $975.00 pair of tourist sandals to replace the $2.00 Havaianas I bought in Brazil last year. I wanted to test it out myself, comparing how wearing something expensive made me feel in contrast to wearing something cheap. As they say, "the proof of the pudding is in the eating." Would the tourist sandals change anything for me?

Did I feel better? Maybe my chest was puffed up for a few days. I was walking around with a grand on my feet, so I can't deny I felt different. But for how long? Not much. I got a few compliments from friends. We had a laugh about it, but that was it. The high from the achievement went away. I moved on. Here's the thing: the idea of buying the sandals was more enjoyable than buying the sandals. The material wealth wasn't what I was after—I was after how I thought it would make me feel. So, once that feeling went away (it always does), I directed my attention to other things (like this book).

Unfortunately, most people can't move on and see it this way. They see material possessions as a representation of their self-worth. If you have it, you're worthy. If you don't have it, you aren't worthy until you do. This is the story that plays around in their heads. So they live life chasing temporary highs, shiny objects, and pride. But they feel drained, unfulfilled. There's a gap in their soul.

These enticing shiny objects and temporary pleasures steal our attention from the tasks that require our attention and focus, and as a result, they delay our progress. Throughout this book, we'll be diving into "advanced attention management" techniques to keep your mind focused on thoughts and actions that matter, and to cut through the noise of illusions.

Consistency Is the Goal

When you measure life through outcomes, you only celebrate success when you reach a significant milestone. You say to yourself, "Once I've accomplished XYZ, I can celebrate." Your mind has worked out a plan for what's going to happen once you achieve your goal—where you'll spend the money, where you'll vacation, what you'll do, etc. This excites our minds, so we focus on it. However, as we've discussed, it represents nothing other than temporary satisfaction in a pocket of time.

When the mind is stuck in the future, you don't have clarity about the present, or about the best next step. Daydreamers accomplish nothing—those who work on the dream do. Once you've identified your Chief Aim, you have to break it down into

Focused Manifesting

small, achievable, present-moment steps, called *Chief Tasks*. If it will take *ten steps* in one direction to reach your goal, then by taking one step at a time, you know for a *fact* you are moving closer to it. If you have multiple big goals, and take steps in different directions, it's hard to measure your progress. You might get busy, but you'll have little to show for all your hard work.

When you have achievable, short-term goals, not only do you have more clarity about your direction, you also narrow your focus. The steadier your progress, the stronger your belief system. What was once a dream becomes more and more a reality. Doubts disappear. Before you know it, you're in a creative, problem-solving flow. You remove the *importance* of achieving the BIG desire by fragmenting it and creating smaller milestones. Consistently taking small steps creates momentum for achieving the bigger goals. For example, there's a difference between writing 500 words every morning and writing 5,000 words now and then. There's a difference between going 100 percent at the gym once every two weeks and going seventy percent three times a week. The former produces growth and momentum, while the latter works with sheer force and luck.

If you wrote 500 words every morning for the next thirty days, you would have 15,000 words in your manuscript. But here's the catch. Sometimes, you'll want to keep writing. One day, you might write 1,000 words (or even 2,000 words). On other days, you might hit that five hundred-word minimum, but it's enough to check that task off your to-do list and feel good about your progress.

If you're looking for the "perfect time" to write 5,000 words in one sitting, you'll find it doesn't come by often. Inspiration doesn't always come to you. Sometimes *you have to go to it*. Most authors don't get inspired to write; they write to get inspired. The same applies to any line of work. If you want to generate ideas and solutions that revolutionize your life path, you need to put yourself in the position to receive that divine guidance.

Here's the biggest difference between focusing on progress and outcomes: *progress doesn't need to be perfect.* It just needs to set the foundation. Outcomes are set in stone, like a number or a physical possession. Focusing only on big, long-term outcomes doesn't create space for inspiration and answers to come to you. By defining a daily goal, you create this space.

As you take steps every day toward achieving your Chief Task, your efforts will result in a large body of work. It's best to manifest pieces of your big desire little by little, as opposed to waiting for the right time and space to do a lot of work in a single day. *Consistency IS the goal.*

Daily Minimum Benchmarks for Alignment

Being consistent in working toward your goals gives you a chance to fine-tune your frequency daily, putting you more and more in alignment with your desires (what we call your Chief Aim). What you want becomes more than a desire; it becomes a frequency with which you resonate. You are one with it. Back in my business consultant days, I used to tell students: *"If you treat your side-hustle like a side-hustle, it'll always be just that. Your side-hustle, nothing more."*

The best way to bring a dream into physical reality is to set daily minimum benchmarks for alignment. These are actions that, once completed, make you feel better and make everything else easier (or unnecessary). The benchmark you assign to yourself on any given day is your Chief Task for that day. All it takes is to move one percent toward your goal every day. If you compound this over a year, you'll be thirty-seven times closer to your goal. However, what does this one percent look like? How do you know when you've completed it?

This is something many people do not address, especially within the personal development space. Without tangible, clear-cut metrics to measure your one percent progress, your manifestation efforts become unreliable. Your attention sways from one task to another, and you spread yourself thin across many tasks instead of focusing on the one you need to give attention to the most. As a result, the Universe responds erratically, delivering a piece of the puzzle you don't need yet, or delivering nothing at all.

This happens because of *a lack of clarity*, which makes it difficult for the mind to know what "finished" looks like. When you have benchmarks established, it's easier to know when you've done enough. Everything from that point on is a bonus. It's easier to give yourself a pat on the back and believe in yourself because you followed through on your plan. These validations create a channel through which the mind can align with the heart. Your thoughts of success match your feelings of success, and that equals *alignment.*

When you feel into the alignment of your heart and mind, your progress becomes tangible and measurable. As you move toward your goal, you notice the headway you are making. The distance between *where you were* to *where you are* creates a feedback loop, strengthening your belief that: "I can achieve this goal."

Even if the results aren't grandiose at first, the distance you have traveled is more than enough evidence to prove you're building something incredible. After weeks or months, it can feel like nothing is happening, but this is when you need to *remain loyal to your ritual,* because when you least expect it, the opportunity will show up. Luck happens when preparation meets opportunity. Remember, the Universe is arranging a million pieces in the background to set you up when the time is right. Your only job is to be ready.

Defining the End

Your Chief Aim comprises a chain of actions that leads you from your point of desire to the point of attainment. If you could take a step back and watch your life as a single event, the mere act of pursuing these minimum daily benchmarks is you *already possessing your desired reality* in an early stage of its development. As author and mystic Neville Goddard would say, "*It is done!*" For example, when you're building a house, you don't just have the idea and it pops into existence. First you dig a hole in the ground, lay the foundation, and build it in layers from there. Over time, when enough action has occurred, the house manifests. But at no single time was the house ever "not a house." It was the house in its early stages of development. There comes a point when the house is complete... and that's the next important idea we need to discuss.

By falling in love with the process and knowing that *what you want already exists*, you remove the importance of achieving it, which liberates you from having to do any chasing. However, you don't want to fall into the trap of always seeking the illusion of perfection, or in modern terms, *perfectionism*. Within our house-building analogy, we understand that the house, despite not having a roof, is still a house. However, just like when builders stop building and declare the house "completed," you need to establish what "done" looks like for your project. If you don't, it's easy to get into the trap of sticking to the same benchmarks day in and day out without ever moving on to the next project. For example, someone can spend years writing a single book, when it should have only taken a few months. Define the end or you'll never reach it.

So, how do you know when you've achieved your goal? When is "the house" completed? The answer will vary depending on the project, but I recommend you plan significant milestones in periods of ninety days. This is the average time to complete a solid project. If you complete it sooner, great. If you delay by a few days or weeks, that's okay, too. However, overall, you want to set goals and milestones that more or less fit this timeline. By the end of the year, you should have taken three to four *massive* leaps toward your long-term vision.

Another way of avoiding perfectionism is by aiming for an eighty percent satisfaction rate. None of your projects will ever feel 100 percent ready. I've written many books, and every time I publish a new one, I feel it could have been a little better. But if I'd continued to tweak it, I would have made it worse. So when you are building or creating anything, avoid diminishing returns. There was a study, published by *The Journal of Behavioral Therapy and Experimental Psychiatry* in 2018, that stated that twenty percent reduced productivity often leads to fifty percent more happiness. How's that for a manifestation technique?

Always keep in mind that your Chief Aim should never be a goal that feels too far ahead in time or unattainable. It needs to be something believable and achievable while still stretching you beyond your comfort zone. This fine balance is another "sweet spot" for achieving focus and flow. The journey to accomplishing your Chief Aim will be riddled with serendipitous moments as the Universe aids you every step of the way. These can come both as blessings and lessons. So always leave room for minor mistakes, delays, and subtle shifts so they don't throw you off track when they come. In world that is changing quickly, being flexible and adaptable are two of the greatest skills you can have. This is just another way of aligning your heart and mind, and as a result, closing the energetic gap between you and "the end."

Vibrational Density

A philosophy I like to follow comes from a quote by the one and only Albert Einstein: "Look deep into nature, and then you will understand everything better." There are many ways of interpreting this quote and applying it to real life, but for simplicity and focus, I'll touch on just one perspective: we'll look at water's transformation between different states, something we all learned in school. Let's start from the top, with water vapor.

When water particles absorb energy (heat), they vibrate faster and break the bonds holding them together. This is called vaporization. It creates the airy, thin appearance of gas. Kind of like your imagination. When you think about an end goal, it's nothing but this transparent, fleeting, substance-less image that comes and goes in your mind.

Focused Manifesting

When the temperature drops, this gas goes through a process called condensation. This is when it rains, or when water vapor transforms into a liquid state. The particles are tightly close together, but not completely. It still flows and shapeshifts to match its environment or its container. This is an excellent state to be in if you're "still trying to figure things out." There's a little more focus than in the previous state. You're no longer a daydreamer, but you also aren't rigid with your path. You've begun testing and experimenting to find solutions that will bring you closer to your goal.

If we drop the temperature and slow the movement of the particles down even more, water undergoes the solidification process. This is when a liquid turns into a solid. Now, the particles are compact. They've settled into a stable arrangement *in the container that holds the ice*.

"But," you might say, "Ryuu, what does all of this mean?"

It means that if you want to turn imagination into reality, you need to put yourself into the *right container* and *limit the space* you have to roam free. By condensing your attention to a single goal, task, and path within a condensed period, you get the right things done in record time, without allowing distractions to pull you away. This is how you turn an airy, fairy dream, into a tangible, living reality. By limiting your energy to a single state and container, you increase your *vibrational density*.

Of course, you don't have to stay in this state forever. It's temporary, and it should come and go in waves. You might dedicate one ninety-day period to one goal and then dedicate the next ninety-days to another goal. Knowing when to make the switch and "solidify" your attention is wisdom that, again, only comes through practice. But if you can master this, creating your dream reality becomes easier.

The concept of vibrational density also follows what's known as "Parkinson's Law." Parkinson's Law is an observation that "Work expands to fill the time available for its completion." Imagine you have an assignment you need to complete by the end of the day. If you work on it in the morning and give yourself the whole day, chances are you'll fill up the day with the task, even if you could have finished it in a few hours. You might take longer breaks, get distracted, or procrastinate because you have this perception that you have plenty of time. Parkinson's Law suggests that often, the time we allocate for a task influences our productivity and efficiency. It's like an invisible force that pushes us to stretch the task out, even if it's unnecessary.

Applying Parkinson's Law can be helpful in achieving your goals because it reminds you to be mindful of how you manage your attention. If you set shorter deadlines or allocate less time for a task, you can avoid unnecessary delays and focus on getting things done more efficiently and in a timelier manner. This doesn't mean you should rush through everything or create unrealistic deadlines. It's about finding the right balance and being conscious of how you use your time to maximize productivity and avoid wasting time.

Therefore, I recommend a ninety-day timeline for your Chief Aim. It's enough time to give you space to make mistakes, but establishes a date by which you have to have everything done. During this "sprint," you condense your attention, and thus, accelerate the process of goal achievement. By bringing yourself back to the present, you become more aware. When you're more aware, you're better able to align yourself with the bigger goals you have for the future.

CHAPTER 2 EXERCISES

Defining the End

What does your reality look like once you've accomplished your Chief Aim? What projects have been completed? Created? Built? Describe it in as much detail as you can.

Defining Daily Minimum Benchmarks for Alignment

Based on your Chief Aim, write down all of the small actions you can take that will bring you closer to completing each of these projects.

Creating Vibrational Density

Break down your Chief Aim into four projects that will be achieved within 3-month intervals. For example: Chief Aim = Build online business; Four Projects = Write a book, build a landing page, create a website, and upload 20 YouTube videos.

CHAPTER 3

THE ARCHITECT OF PERCEPTION

Law #3: Your Environment Creates You

"You cannot heal in the same environment in which you got sick."

Unknown

Law of Attraction teachers often mention that our internal reality creates our external reality. This is because of the fractal nature of the Universe—everything is a mirror image of everything else, into infinity. But this principle also works in reverse, especially for those who are unaware of this mechanism. Things in our external world can influence our internal world and can change the thoughts we think, the emotions we feel, and the actions we take—if we allow it.

Ancient masters and mystics agreed on this principle. As stated in Hermetic teachings, "As above, so below. As below, so above." External stimuli play a vital role in how our internal world operates. The environments you engage in change the way you operate in the world. And this is the basis of this chapter—understanding that the places you frequent have a direct effect on *how you focus*, and as a result, they affect the realities you attract. Of course, you still have the power to change your perspective, independent of the shape the external world takes. However, understand this: your subconscious mind is *always* capturing the information your environment projects.

We cannot forget we are still human beings, with animal instincts and innate survival mechanisms. Whether we like it or not, our environment will always play a part in the engineering of our inner world. That being said, in a world riddled with distraction, one of the most powerful ways of aligning yourself with your Chief Aim is by shifting the dynamics of your day-to-day environment.

The Foundation of Perceived Reality

When we're children, we're taught about our five senses. We categorize our senses into their own little boxes and understand that this is the way we interpret the world. However, most people don't think deeply about how each sense operates and how they work together. While it's true that each sense has its own function, your experience of reality is a beautiful blend of these senses, creating the illusion you experience in any given moment. Let me explain: You're not just reading this book. You're holding it in your hands, in a unique environment, hearing sounds that differ from any other place on this planet. The time of day dictates the degree of light around you, which affects the hues of colors you perceive. The smells, the tastes, the feelings you have all communicate on a molecular level with your organism, informing your reality and generating your mood, vibration, and *focus*.

Being alive is a wild, miraculous experience. Our senses sustain our reality in such a way that we get immersed in an illusion we believe is real. What is our reality? It's not just what we see, hear, smell, taste, or feel...there is much more happening at the cellular, molecular, and atomic levels we cannot perceive. The "surface level" information our senses provide feeds back into our lives. When someone shouts, we become alert. When clothes are itchy, we're distracted by the discomfort. When it's too dark to see, we turn on the lights. Our senses influence our decisions.

If you're working on a specific project, for example, while surrounded by papers, notifications, and people who are focusing on other projects, getting distracted is inevitable. To prevent this, you need to isolate your senses into little bubbles of focused energy. When everything you watch and listen to reminds you of your Chief Aim, it's impossible not to move toward it. What's important to remember is that *your senses are the first generator of experience*. They sustain the illusion of your perceived reality, and when you understand this is an area you can influence with your will, you can tap into deeper layers of manifesting and reality creation.

Ontological Design

The environments you come into contact with influence your decisions and your behaviors, and may either enhance or limit your ability to manifest your dream life. This is the underlying principle of Ontological Design, which, in layperson's terms, describes the idea that *humans design the world and the world designs humans.* Through their will, humans change the dynamics of their environment, which in turn affects the inner engineering of the humans living in those environments. A perfect example is your social circle. You become attached to the people you have chosen (either consciously or unconsciously) to surround yourself with, and these people can either hold you back or raise you to new standards. By designing your social circle, you can design where the vast majority of your focus goes.

Focused Manifesting

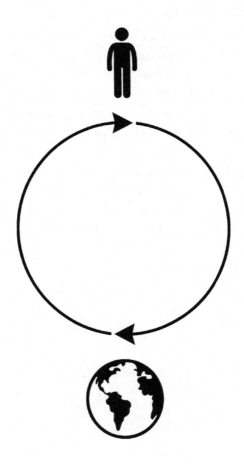

Imagine if every day, as you wake up, you see a poster on your bedroom wall that reads, "You're going to fail again today, so why bother even trying?" How would that affect your day? Would you wake up with a spring in your step or would you grunt at the unbearable weight of the world? While you don't need to place motivational posters all over your house, becoming mindful of your environment can unveil a lot of hidden causes behind your inner (and outer) reality. Your environment is a perfect mirror in which you can see areas that might need more attention.

You can optimize your spaces to support the most productive, focused, and positive version of you. When it comes to changing your state of being, a lot of the heavy lifting can come from changing your physical environment. A vast majority of the population underrate how powerful an effect this can have. For example, it is not as inspirational to wake up each day to a room filled with unfolded clothes, unpaid bills, disorganized papers, and undisposed-of junk scattered everywhere as it is waking up to a tidy, organized room. Which one of these two scenarios feeds the reality that you're an organized person who has their life together? Which of these two-room descriptions gives you the space and energy to focus on just one goal?

Everyone knows the answer, yet we get caught up in our lives and forget that these minor elements come together in a big way. Our personal space is the foundation of our personal reality and therefore, it's one of the most practical aspects you can change to get into alignment with the achievement of your Chief Aim.

Sensory Design Audit

Once we understand the principle of Ontological Design, the next step is to audit the spaces in your reality: your living, office, social, and digital spaces—any place or thing with which your senses come into contact. By weaving your Chief Aim into these spaces, it becomes easier to align yourself with its achievement. Better choices, more opportunities, and periods of deep focus can all come when you design your environment to be organized and inspirational.

Focused Manifesting

The first layer of change should occur in the places you spend most of your time. For example, if you work at an unfulfilling job inside a cubicle from nine to five and are attempting to grow your own business, start by introducing components into your space that fuel your new focus. Declutter your space of anything that discourages your new focus. For example, remove large piles of paper, organize your files, and cut back that suffocating to-do list. Reduce as much as you can. In this new space, you can add a journal to record new ideas, a plant to remind you of growth, and a to-do list that contains at least one high-leverage activity that moves you toward your dream.

The technique you use to declutter and refocus your life doesn't matter. The important step is that you're redefining the space. You can introduce everything from essential oils for sparking inspiration to binaural beats to stay dialed-in on the work you're doing. It's important to extend this practice not only to your physical spaces, but to your digital ones as well. If you're spending a lot of time swiping random videos all day, you should at the very least create feeds with content that inspires you to work on your goals. When I first got started on this journey, I deleted my personal Instagram account, where I followed all my childhood friends, and started a new one where I only followed successful people in my field who were living the life I wanted.

However, the most optimal way of doing this is to delete your socials altogether (unless it's to create content). If you're going to consume content, refrain from anything that is short and dopamine-spiking (like scrolling on social media). Instead, consume long-form content. Read books and watch podcasts. Although reels and shorts can give you little snippets of sound advice, a lot of them lack context, depth, or nuance, and have the sole purpose of going viral and attracting as much attention as possible.

We need to accept that we aren't hermits living in caves. We need somewhere to put our attention, we need topics to discuss, and we need people with whom to discuss them. When you optimize the content you consume, you realize how much of your life needs to change, from the people you spend time with, to the type of work you do. This takes time and requires you to discern *good* information from the *right* information. However, once you have decided on your favorite podcast hosts or authors, it becomes easier to embody the traits, actions, and focus they talk about. But don't get too caught up with what others are discussing either. Remember, practical, personal experience will always be more valuable than theoretical ideas.

Look at your physical and digital spaces as empty canvases and start designing them to match your newly found Chief Aim. This is how you leverage your environment to influence your decisions, behaviors, and attitudes. Start with minor changes. For example, once you decide on the one task you are going to do at work tomorrow, prepare your office the night before so when you walk in, you're all set to focus. From there, work your way up to more difficult layers, like putting a pause on a relationship or letting go of negative friends so you can give attention to more positive relationships (like an accountability partner or a mastermind buddy).

The more you work on optimizing your environment, the more it compounds. The content you consume can inspire an innovative idea. The new environments you frequent can attract opportunities out of the blue. Your mastermind buddy can recommend a quality resource to grow your business. And it's all because you're giving energy to the dream by changing your environment. When you give energy to the dream, it grows, and within a supportive environment, the growth feels exponential.

This is alignment!

The ancient Chinese understood this concept—they practiced what mystics call *geomancy* (or what is more commonly referred to as *Feng Shui*).

Aligning the Energies of Your Space

Within the Feng Shui model of reality, everything has *chi* or *energy*. Modern physics echoes this belief, claiming that everything comprises vibration. According to Chinese Feng Shui, how you organize your space affects the flow of this chi energy. But chi isn't just energy. It is *life force energy*, and it's responsible for manifesting everything in your world. Therefore, if the chi of your environment is out of alignment with the Chief Aim you're looking to manifest, prepare to experience a lot of resistance. Implementing the core principles of Feng Shui can give you guidance about the energy side of Ontological design and how the energy of your environment can influence your ability to focus.

Clear Out the Clutter

The first concept you can apply universally is that of decluttering your space. This includes *all* of your spaces. The environments you live in, work in, socialize in, and connect to digitally. The easiest way to find your focus is to have fewer things to focus on. The more elements in your life you can remove, the more attention you can give to the elements that matter. When you have a lot of elements stealing, asking, and begging for your attention, it's difficult to stay focused. Whenever I have periods where I want to engage in deep work, I reduce the number of events I attend, the people I see, and the activities in which I engage. I keep it simple. If you have a bunch of events scheduled this month, twenty friends you need to connect with every week, and a daily routine packed with activities, your attention is diluted. Less is more.

When you live minimally, you give yourself space to define and discover the elements that are important to you. What are the events and activities that will lead you closer to your Chief Aim? Who are the people who will support your goals? Making your life minimal also allows you to see areas of your life that were draining your energy. When life is too busy, it's difficult to notice what is stealing your attention, because your senses are on overload and your mind is busy processing incoming information. When you scatter your attention, it is difficult to channel insight. *Open up space in your life to receive guidance.*

If you think about your clutter like data in a computer, you can imagine that every object of focus that comes into contact with your senses occupies processing power. This means that the more items and people you have around, the more disorder there will be within your spaces—and to stay present, you will need a greater investment of energy. When everything is in its place, clean, and tidy, your mind can recognize the task at hand and can stay focused on completing it.

When you declutter physically, you're also decluttering mentally. Following the principles of Ontological Design, one leads to the other. Therefore, I encourage you to look at the environments you frequent throughout your day. What can you reduce, eliminate, or declutter?

Tackle the Biggest Mess First

At one point in our lives, every one of us has had that *thing* that's been piling up for weeks, months, and sometimes years. This

Focused Manifesting

is the work of *entropy*, Nature's tendency to move toward chaos and disorder. The bigger it gets, the more intimidating it is to tackle. So, most people never tackle it. We do nothing to diminish its overwhelming nature. We leave it to build up over time, draining the energy of the environment, renting space in the back of our minds, and deteriorating the quality of the space. When handling your clutter monsters, you have to approach them differently than you would washing dishes or taking out the recycling. This type of clutter requires conviction and action so bold you're willing to sacrifice your weekend to tackle it once and for all. Small intentions don't work. Small actions keep you stuck. The key is to block out a day or more to make decluttering your primary focus. This requires you to invest your time, energy, and sometimes money, but it will be more worth it than you could ever imagine.

Right Now Is the Perfect Time

How do we keep from going into battle with these monsters of clutter? In our lives, we're already required to be vigilant with certain types of clutter. Taking out the trash, sweeping the porch, doing the laundry, washing your dishes after eating—these tiny investments of energy can wear a person down. If you've had a challenging day, it's easy to tell yourself, "I'll do it in the morning!" as you fade into oblivion. Except, in the morning, you are in a rush... and you keep putting the task off until one day, you come home to a pile of laundry, dirty dishes piled sky high, and a fridge full of sad-looking vegetables.

Here's the thing. While doing a minor task might seem like a hassle, the truth is that those tasks are *easiest in the moment* and become more difficult as time passes. The bigger it gets, the more it will beg for your attention. If it's a task that will take less than five minutes—just do it. Get it out of your mind and free up your processing power so you can focus on the important things. As noted earlier, disorder from entropy leads to more clutter, so get yourself into the habit of decluttering and organizing your space.

Naturally, with every completed task, you're telling your mind that you're a "go getter," that you don't leave things to stagnate. You keep moving. You're active. You're engaged! Wherever you go, you influence your environment. Use your victory over your environment as your first confirmation of your new reality.

The Law of the Vacuum

When it comes to changing your environment, it doesn't happen by chance, and it isn't a one-and-done deal. It requires constant maintenance and adjusting. Reality will always throw new obstacles, distractions, and thoughts at you to fill up the space you're creating. This is *the law of the vacuum.* This law states that nature abhors a vacuum. It dislikes empty space. When you remove something from your life, you're giving nature the opportunity to fill it up. Now, most people don't know how to use this mechanism to their advantage. They'll declutter their space, and within a few days or weeks, they'll clutter it up again.

The mind follows this tendency, too. You can meditate all you want, sit in silence for hours, and neutralize every thought that crosses your mind. However, Nature will not fold. It'll introduce you to a whole new collection of thoughts and stories to fill up that space. If you're not intentional about designing your world, it'll be designed for you. If you're not intentional about filling your space, it'll be filled for you. Create your life, or it will create itself by default.

Clutter will always build. Thoughts will always come. Therefore, our job is to guide reality by filling our spaces with good elements that raise our vibration. Create an environment that rewards productive behavior, motivates positive thinking, and makes you feel good. I don't use this word often, but this is a literal *hack*.

When you surround yourself with positive, supportive energy, achieving the Chief Aim you set out to manifest is inevitable. It doesn't happen overnight, but as you make changes to your environment, reality will pick up the cues. What you once thought was difficult to attract floods your reality. So much so you need to cut out even excellent opportunities if it means attracting and staying focused on better ones.

Take back control of your environment. When you do, everything you need will show up. When you become the architect of your own perception, you integrate new beliefs and new potential into your life. Before you know it, you're acting, thinking, and feeling like the 2.0 version of yourself—the version that takes action, attracts opportunities, and builds the reality you've always wanted. It's not a passive process. Rearranging where you work, connecting with people on a similar path, cutting out negative friends, and being responsible for maintaining and optimizing your new environment are just a few things you can do.

In the next chapter, we're going to take a closer look at optimizing your personal spaces so you can develop an unshakeable focus and a blissful relationship with your work.

CHAPTER 3 EXERCISES

Decluttering

Write down a list of environments you need to declutter. This can include living, working, social, and digital spaces.

Tackle The Biggest Mess First

Between all of these environments, which one is the most cluttered?

Focused Manifesting

Schedule

If it's not scheduled, it's not real. Create an event in your calendar to tackle this environment before moving onto the next chapter.

CHAPTER 4

SPACES OF REALITY

Law #4: Less Is More

"The secret to happiness is not found in seeking more, but in developing the capacity to enjoy less."

Socrates

Focused Manifesting

In the last chapter, we covered the importance of managing our environment and what comes into contact with our senses, applying and optimizing the principle of Ontological Design. In this chapter, we'll take this one step further, redefining the spaces you want to be a part of, removing the fluff that fogs your vision, and liberating yourself from *the trap of materialism*. By doing this, you will focus on essentials and maintain a prime state of being. Too many of us need physical manifestations to prove our worth. To prove that we're capable. To prove that we're on the right path. But this mentality is backward, and soon you'll find out why. Now we're going to look at how to create an empowering workspace so you can get the most out of your work.

Many people don't like to work. Their workspace is uninviting, disorganized, and intimidating. It's no wonder they have a difficult time staying focused and completing tasks. If this sounds like you, applying the principles outlined below will eradicate any misalignment you may have.

Redefine Comfort

In Western society, most people believe that more "things" will bring more comfort. They accumulate objects they desire and fill their homes with toys, ornaments, tchotchkes, and props from all over the world. However, no matter how much they invest, these objects never fill the hole inside them. It turns out no matter how much money you spend collecting items that are supposed to prove your luxury and status, none of them fill your soul.

Many people know this at a fundamental level, but when it comes to living it, few understand, leading them to chase money, fame, and recognition. They believe that when they achieve X-amount of money in their bank account, they'll allow themselves to feel X emotion. The more I've studied the ways of monks, the more I've realized we don't need expensive things to be happy or even comfortable. When you adopt a simple lifestyle, you'll have more money, time, and energy to invest in expanding the abundance you already have, instead of wasting it trying to prove yourself to others.

It's a common misconception that when you make money, you need to spend it on luxury items. However, I've also noticed that many of the wealthiest people in the world keep their possessions to a bare minimum. Warren Buffet still lives in his \$31,000 home in Omaha, Nebraska that he bought over 50 years ago. Amacio Ortega, the founder of Zara, lives in a discreet apartment in La Coruña, Spain with his wife, while they frequent their favorite coffee shop as opposed to high-end luxury restaurants. They spend their money consciously. They don't spend it on trying to prove anything to anyone. In fact, if they could, they'd prefer a low profile. Of course, there are exceptions, however, the most common pattern I've noticed is that the richer people get, the less they try to show it.

If we're to follow Neville Goddard's most popularized principle, "live in the end," it's safe to say that if we want to tune into the frequency of abundance and wealth, we shouldn't be spending more, we should spend *less*. We should delay our acquisition of luxuries like mansions and fancy cars for when they cost a fraction of what we earn, instead of more than half our yearly income.

People who live far below their means enjoy a freedom that people busy upgrading their lifestyles can't fathom.

Naval Ravikant

Focused Manifesting

Spending less on luxuries follows the common concept of *delayed gratification*. This is the idea of delaying an ego-driven impulse today for a more expansive, abundant tomorrow. Invest in assets that will compound your growth over time instead of in liabilities that give you small, temporary jolts of pride. There was a famous study conducted by psychologist Walter Mischel at Stanford University that shone a light on this concept. He put ninety kids in a room at a table and placed one sugary marshmallow in front of each child. The children knew that if they waited fifteen minutes without eating the marshmallow, the psychologist would reward them with a second one. After recording the tests, and tracking the kids throughout their lives, they noticed that the kids who waited out the fifteen minutes had a higher tendency for success in life. Interesting, right? But, this study has since been debunked. Another researcher reported that in fact, the kids' ability to be successful as adults had nothing to do with their ability to wait out the fifteen minutes, it had to do with *the environment they grew up in*. The kids who tested high in patience came from wealthier homes. The kids who grew up in less fortunate families showed signs that they were impatient. Now, does this mean you're doomed if you come from a low-income family? Of course not. But this study does prove two concepts:

1. the importance of having a supportive environment, and

2. the researchers linked the children's ability to delay gratification with whether the child had experienced abundance in their upbringing or not.

When you can train yourself to embody the trait of delaying gratification and create an environment that nurtures it, you realizing success is just a matter of time. Why spend time around people who like to spend money when you can spend time around people who like to grow it?

62

There are many reasons we fall into the trap of instant gratification. Aside from ego-driven desires like status and power, one common contributing factor is the digital nature of our reality. Mobile devices have made everything more accessible. By tapping a few buttons, you can buy anything you want in a matter of seconds. As a result, we've conditioned our brains to want to experience a dopamine spike in all things—whether it's acquiring stuff, starting a business, or having a relationship. But we soon discover that chasing short-term pleasures leads to fleeting satisfaction that soon vanishes. This chase comes from a place of lack, and not of abundance.

When you incorporate *the law of less is more* into your life, you'll notice life slow down—in a good way. You won't be so occupied with maintaining and consuming. Instead, you will build and create. Here are a few techniques to help:

Focused Manifesting

1) Spend Less Than You Earn

You would think this is obvious, but considering that less than twenty-five percent of all households in the U.S. are debt-free, and that forty million Americans carry credit card or student loan debt—spending less than you earn is not simple. In our consumer economy, getting pre-approved credit cards is as easy as getting a sunburn at the beach. However, when you audit your budget and spend less than you earn, you have a bit more "economic power." Cash builds up. You have disposable income to invest. Your fear of having a random accident or not being able to pay bills dissipates. *You live in a different version of comfort.*

On my travels, I made a good friend, Matt, who works as a bartender for higher-end lounges in Colorado. Many of his friends do similar work. However, because his friends live beyond their means, they're stuck working in one location, year-round, without ever experiencing any real financial or personal growth in their lives. All the while, Matt travels often, gets decent annual returns from his investments, and designs his life the way he wants. He prioritized freedom and flexibility over material goods and status.

Of course, this is just one example and one way of doing it, but it proves my point: it doesn't matter what stage of the journey you're in. If you define what's important to you, and prioritize it, you can experience it more often. If you're always finding yourself short on funds at the end of the month, perhaps it's time to dive into your finances. Where you can you cut expenses? If you have to live below your means for a few months to gain an advantage, so be it. Don't let ego-driven desires stop you from building and manifesting your dream.

The quickest path to your greatest, most ambitious goals is often the longest one. Start building now.

2)   Own Less to Manage Less

As I said earlier about clutter, everything you own requires a level of "processing power." All our stuff takes up attention. We spend energy thinking about when, where, and how we're going to use these items. The ego needs to keep in the back of its mind the story that you "own" this or that. When you possess a lot of material things, you're identifying with it.

"I own this hat."

"This hat is mine."

"It's my hat, not yours."

"I bought this hat for me."

Whether we like to believe it or not, the more possession we have, the more identified we are with our ego and reality. The more you own, the more responsibility you have. These possessions require your care, maintenance, and attention. If you don't give something attention, over time it either collects dust (and energy), or you end up feeling like you "wasted money" and you use it just to use it.

If I don't use an item at least a few times a year, it's not worth owning. Too many of us hoard possessions like we're stuck in cave-dweller times. Last month, I visited a house in Los Angeles that was cluttered. The garage was huge, but the only space it had was a narrow trail to the washing machine. I felt like I was in a jungle of junk. The room in front of the one I was staying in, was surrounded by hundreds of law books that have been collecting dust for over twenty years. The kitchen had so many machines on the counter that there was barely enough space to make a sandwich.

When you live in environments like this, it has a *massive* effect on your ability to receive new blessings and manifestations. When you declutter, you're telling the Universe, "I'm ready to receive." But until that time comes, you'll just keep experiencing the same stagnant energy that's a clear reflection of your environment.

3) Keep It Simple

People like to overcomplicate goal-achievement. Most people believe they know how their manifestation is going to work out. But we can't control reality. We can only guide it in the general direction we want it to go. The best way to do this is to keep the process as simple as possible. When you worry or overindulge in a process, it's because you're overcomplicating it. This leads people to not trust others to handle specific tasks, to take on more than they can handle, and to turn their life into one busy mess. Learning to let go of complexity comes with learning to *let go of control.*

Over-complicating things can be rooted in a desire to feel in control. We add more elements than we need, say more than we need to say, and do more than we need to do. Doing this fogs your ability to make solid, efficient decisions. You spread your attention thin and never make significant progress. The key is to simplify. *Occam's Razor* is a principle that states that the best solution to any problem is often the simplest one. Simplification starts with your environment. If your schedule is overcomplicated, your life will be overcomplicated. The more you need to think about what you need to do, the more energy you will spend. The common terminology for this is *decision fatigue*. When you make many decisions, their quality diminishes throughout the day. The more you simplify your daily life, the easier it is to make the right decisions that lead to the right outcomes. Do not get addicted to the dopamine of busyness and complexity. That will overload your attention with nonsense that halts your progress and evolution.

Building Your Room of Creation

Until this point, we've covered a good chunk of the relationship between your ability to manifest and your environment, and how what you own can dilute your energy and distract you from your goals.

Knowing how to focus is the foundation of success. If you have any hope of creating a meaningful, impactful, sustainable career or business, you're going to need a space that inspires depth, creativity, and focus. Manifesting any successful project results from discipline and funneling your imagination. This is an art. It requires you to exercise your creativity while limiting it.

Let's build what I like to call your *Room of Creation*. Of course, many people call it their "office space," "workspace," or "desk." It's the same *space,* and for manifesting your desired reality, *you're going to need one.*

> *"To create without freedom is difficult, without limits, impossible."*
>
> My tattoo artist, Marcelo

It doesn't matter how many good ideas you have or how much of a genius you think you are, if you can't find the time to shape your thoughts, they won't evolve. You need to put pen to paper. One

Focused Manifesting

way to do this is to by finding an environment that both keeps you *creative* and leads to *creation*. How do you do this? Start by creating an inviting environment. Look at your workspace—whether it's an entire room or just a corner of a table—you want to create a space that invites you to sit down and get to work. One of the easiest ways to achieve this is to keep your work area as tidy as possible. Of course, when you're lost in the art of creation and riding the wave of inspiration, your work area will get cluttered again. The key is to get into the habit of *neutralizing your workspace* at the end of each day.

This means organizing your papers, closing all your tabs, shutting down all your windows, putting away your office supplies, and bringing it all back to square one. When you do this, you give yourself permission the next day to be creative because now, you have room to fill! Remember the vacuum of reality. If you don't create the space for the creativity to flow, you'll feel congested, cluttered, and stuck.

When you look at your workspace, it's important that you *feel empowered*. Audit the direction you're facing. What's behind your computer? What's behind you? How can you rearrange or improve the layout of the space so you feel inspired, focused, and directed toward your goal? For example, I like to work facing the door of whatever room I'm in. I find I can't immerse myself if I have my back to the entrance/exit of the room. Some people need to be surrounded by other people who are also working and focused. I prefer to isolate myself.

When you find a configuration that works for you, take advantage of it. Create as much as you can. However, be mindful that your preferences will change. There's a downside to being *too* disciplined with your workspace. In fact, by rearranging your workspace every few months, you increase your ability to maintain a flow state. If your creativity feels stagnant, change something about your environment.

Don't overthink this. You don't want to use "optimizing my environment" as an excuse to not get to work. I worked with a client who used the "I'm still decluttering" excuse as the reason they weren't doing the work. Fun fact: You're *always* going to be decluttering. At the end of every day. That's entropy. It's Nature.

The important questions to ask yourself are: *How does this workspace make me feel? Does it inspire me to work and stay focused? Does it tune me into the right frequency?* If not, change it to get it closer to that feeling, no matter how small.

Digital Alignment

It's impossible to go through life today without technology. Many people fantasize about "getting away from it all" so they can "reconnect with their spirit," thinking that only then will they find the peace they seek. Although these digital detox moments are important, they're not the only solution. Our lives are immersed in technology, and we've become so dependent on it that to dream of a life without technology is folly. It's only going to become more prevalent in our lives. This means that instead of trying to distance yourself from it, *digital alignment* would be more effective.

Digital alignment means redefining the purpose of your technology. *If you don't give the technology you use a purpose, it will give you one.* We've reached this stage, but unfortunately, most people are unaware of it. The vast majority of humanity is *under the spell of technology*, trapped in "euphoric slumber." The mind is happy because it has an infinite number of distractions and dopamine spikes. It becomes impossible to get bored because there's always a new notification, a new video, or a new app asking for your attention.

Technology gives us the opportunity to experience a reality we're not experiencing physically. You can have followers or subscribers but have no human connection. You can explore the world but can't breathe the fresh air of the exotic locations you are seeing on your screen. If you're not careful, all that stimuli can affect your state of being. If you want to manifest your dream life, manage your technology. As I mentioned earlier, start by *ascribing purpose to your devices.* For example, why do you need a smartphone? Communication? Documentation? Content creation? Entertainment? Leisure?

Your smartphone is a miraculous thing. It gives you a camera, a recording device, instant communication globally, knowledge about any subject, and with added apps, you can balance budgets, plan projects, edit pictures, etc. All of this on a tiny device that fits in your pocket. By giving your smartphone a purpose, no matter what it is, you narrow your focus and avoid losing yourself whenever you use it. When you have fifty-plus lit-up apps to choose from, half of them sporting a red notification, dings coming every few minutes, it's impossible to not let them distract you. Digital alignment begins by giving your device a purpose, and then decluttering it to fit that purpose. For example, if you want to use your smartphone to communicate and network, you need to delete any app that doesn't fit this description.

Personally, I dislike having work on my phone. I found out that whenever I was out with friends or family, and I received an email or message about work, I removed myself from the moment. Since then, I've deleted every work-related app from my phone. If you give a device, like your phone or computer, more than one purpose, invest in another device that can fulfill the second purpose. If you watch Netflix on the same device on which you do deep technical work, you're putting yourself in a position to be pulled away from the activity you're trying to focus on. It's like asking a child to do homework in the playground.

By giving your devices one purpose, you're priming yourself to focus on one thing, as opposed to leaving yourself open to being distracted. When you give any device more than one purpose, you're more likely to switch between functions and dilute your energy. This can stop you from focusing on a task you need to work on and stop you from being present with something you're trying to enjoy. *If you want to live a full life, learn to focus fully.*

Another way of optimizing your digital environment is by decorating it and sprinkling messages everywhere. For example, create a vision board on your lock screen or have an inspirational video as your screensaver. Change your passwords to mini positive affirmations or rename your folders with your goals. Just as you have designed your physical space to align all your attention toward achieving your Chief Aim, design your digital space that way as well. When you immerse yourself in the vision you have for your life, it becomes impossible not to move toward it.

While technology is hypnotizing billions of people on the planet, those who have turned it into a creation tool are leveraging it to their best advantage. Now that you understand the importance of optimizing your spaces, both physical and digital, it's time to move to a higher dimension of influence… it's time for an audit of your social life.

CHAPTER 4 EXERCISES

Spending Less

Review your monthly expenses. Where are you unconsciously overspending? Write down a list of expenses you can reduce or eliminate to create more financial ease.

_____

_____

_____

_____

Owning Less

Review your belongings. What do you own too much of? Write down a list of belongings you can reduce, discard, or donate to create space for more manifestations.

_____

_____

_____

_____

Room of Creation

Where do you work? Write down a list of ways you can make this space more inviting and inspiring.

Digital Alignment

Write down a list of all the technology you use. Next to each, write down its primary purpose. Then optimize each (deleting/downloading apps) to match this purpose.

CHAPTER 5

SOCIAL SYNERGY

Law #5: Your Circle Creates You

"The better you are at surrounding yourself with people of high potential, the greater your chance for success."

John C. Maxwell

Since the beginning of their evolution, human beings have always been dependent on one another for survival. The people in our lives have a significant impact on our state of being and our ability to manifest. If you have a loving, supportive, encouraging social environment that complements the success you want to attract, success becomes inevitable. Imagine having a network that reminds you of why you started and where you're going every single day. Imagine if every person with whom you interact with gives *you energy* instead of draining it from you. Of course, this won't be the case all the time because we're human and prone to making mistakes. We spend time doing things we shouldn't. But, this doesn't mean you can't put the intention out there to optimize your network.

When I got started on my entrepreneurship journey, I felt alone. There was nobody I could talk to about my business or with whom I could bounce ideas around—not my university professors, coworkers, family, and not even my closest friends. It felt like nobody understood my new path. Nobody was excited about it like I was. It was me and a bunch of online video recordings. But everything changed when I immersed myself in communities that complimented my new direction. It started off with brief introductions and questions I posted in online groups. Then I'd exchange personal messages back and forth with people through socials. Then I'd get together with people on one-on-one Zoom calls. I was invited to take part in weekly group calls. Friendships blossomed. This led to in-person meet ups, masterminds, and trips around the world. From there, I was invited to join communities and groups that were in alignment with my values.

My network expanded. I wasn't alone anymore. Most of the people I keep in touch with nowadays understand my mission and are supportive of it. If they don't understand it, they're at the very least supportive, and are still a good friend to have. Getting connected with people who have a purpose, who engage in high-vibration activities, and who love to live life became a new normal for me. Naturally, this integrated with my sense of identity. The people I talk with the most are living their best lives, so it's only normal that I resonate with that frequency, too. Your circle creates you, so make sure it's a good one.

Maybe you don't have the circle of your dreams right now. Most people are reluctant to change their circle, and that's because instinctually, we fear rejection and loneliness. When enquiring for relationship advice, it's common to hear that you should "cut everyone out." But that's not always as simple as it seems.

In this chapter, we're going to dive into the dynamics of social circles in three different pillars: Your Inner, Mastermind, and Mentor Circles. Inside each, we'll categorize the relationships that provide you with a balanced network that feeds the dream you want to manifest.

The Origin of Distractions

Where do distractions come from? I've reflected on this question many times over the years. The Universe has many unique ways of pushing and pulling us in multiple directions, often in moments when we least expect them. They move us out of alignment, flood our minds with thoughts, agitate our emotions, and make us feel manipulated.

These universal forces are known as *pendulums*. The pendulum concept was coined by author Vadim Zeland, who wrote the book *Reality Transurfing*. In his book, he describes pendulums as invisible energetic thought structures that are spread across the field (a field of information that exists beyond space and time). Pendulums, as we normally think of them, are two-legged structures that have a string hanging from the middle with a ball attached to the end that swings back and forth.

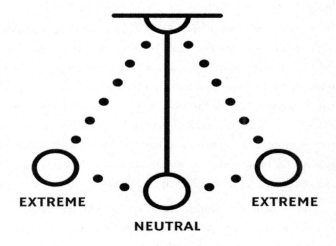

In Zeland's book, the base of the pendulum represents ideologies, ideas, doctrines, organizations, or beliefs that survive based on the energy their cohort of followers (whether supporters or fanatics) provide. Each pendulum has what's known as a resonant frequency associated with it that determines the rhythm of the swing. The way someone gets hooked by a pendulum is by tuning into its resonant frequency.

Pendulums hook people through polarization. When you're hooked, you either hate or love the ideology. You are either for or against the idea. Either way, you're feeding energy to the pendulum and losing complete freedom of thought. Your thoughts are now being directed by this external force. At this stage, you've lost neutral balance, the balance necessary to make conscious choices that move you in the direction of most happiness and fulfillment.

Pendulums divert you from your path by manipulating negative energy and taking advantage of emotions like fear, guilt, and resentment, etc. By instigating certain emotions, pendulums can move large groups of people to either attract them (draining their energy) or destroy them (neutralizing their influence).

If it weren't for the energy we feed to pendulums, they wouldn't exist. For example, ancient hunter-gatherer populations practiced totemism and animism, spiritual beliefs in which they worshipped totem animals or aspects of nature as the seen and unseen powers that orchestrated the rhythms of life. Over time, with the advent of education, totemism and animism died out—or, we can say that the totemism and animism pendulums died. These pendulums were replaced with other religions, social mores, laws, community codes of conduct, etc.—each of them a pendulum unto itself.

Throughout the world, there are an infinite number of pendulums, each having its own unique agenda. For example, consider the pendulum of a football team. Everyone who supports a specific team has a similar thought process about the team. They wear team colors, sport team logos on their clothing, and chant team slogans. When their team scores, everyone cheers. When the team loses, everyone frowns. The team flourishes, earns money, and gains influence as long as there are fans to support it. Now, say there is one neutral individual in a stadium full of supporters of one team. That individual will *follow the crowd*, picking up on the other fans' thoughts and behaviors based on the team's performance. That individual just joined the pendulum.

Now, pendulums can have a multitude of effects, and can influence you in more ways than just through the affinities of crowds of people. In fact, most, if not every belief system in our society is a pendulum. However, for the sake of simplicity (and the theme of this chapter), let's break them down through the perspective of people. An ideology or idea (like a football team) may only have a slight effect on your state and attention. The real challenge comes when you find out *who* is supporting them and *how many people* are supporting them.

Are you willing to be the "odd person out?" Will you open yourself up to learning these new sets of rules, cultural tendencies, and behaviors so you can fit in with the crowd? The answer to these questions will depend on how hooked you are to the pendulum. If you're in a twenty-plus-year relationship with a person who is fanatic about a team, taking part in the event may seem like a good idea to strengthen the relationship. If you just met someone and they invited you to a game, rejecting the invitation won't be such a big deal.

By nature, every pendulum follows a set of principles, systems, and ideologies—a set script if you will—within each pendulum there is a deeper current that is not expressed openly. There are "hidden agendas" in each one. These agendas are constructive, destructive, or neutral.

A constructive pendulum will pull you up, shift your identity, and help you move closer to your goals. This type of pendulum, although having an agenda it follows, can still be of benefit to the stage you're at in your journey. In my own life, an example of constructive pendulums are the masterminds I join. Although I lose complete freedom of thought, the energy of the group helps me expand my mind and bring me to the next level in my development.

Then there are neutral pendulums. One neutral pendulum that comes to mind is the government education system. It doesn't distract me because it has nothing to do with my path. It's not for me, and that's that. A neutral pendulum is one that has no say in your reality and that you simply ignore. Other people might see it as an opportunity to pursue a successful career, and in such a case, that pendulum could be beneficial for them. However, if you don't know what you want, and are floating around, the education system could lure you in with promises it can't keep—potentially making it a destructive pendulum and pulling you down.

The fact that much of society follows the traditional education path makes it even more alluring. People give their attention, money, and energy to a system they're not even sure will benefit them, until they have been through it. Once they end up with that degree, only then will they be able to determine the value the pendulum brought to their lives. As a constructive pendulum, the education system may well help you launch a new career. Or, as a destructive pendulum, it could manifest as debt and an unfulfilling career path.

If you're unclear about *who you are* and *what you want*, you could fall prey to a destructive pendulum—you could be relying on pure luck to carry you through life.

There is no way to escape the world of pendulums. Look at any system operating around you—social, cultural, political, governmental, religious, ethical, etc., break it down to its component parts and you will find a pendulum. While it might be an abstract concept for some people to grasp, if you remind yourself that these entities exist, you have power to disengage from them. The practice of "quieting the mind" can help you detach from the pendulums with which you are unconsciously engaged with. When you are mindful of your thoughts, you become more clear about your true desires, rather than allowing yourself to be influenced by ideologies that do not serve your higher purpose.

While I could continue in great detail about the influence of pendulums on society and our lives, we're going to bring it closer to home. With this introduction to pendulums, let's analyze how they relate to your social circles and your ability to manifest.

The Influence of Pendulums

By understanding pendulums, it becomes easier to notice the psychosocial effects our environment has on our ability to manage our attention and attract the life we want. It's no surprise that when we surround ourselves with the right people, doing, learning, and thinking the right way feels effortless. But this is easier said than done. We're all born into a particular family dynamic, raised around a certain group of people, and influenced by a unique cultural norm. We have no control over this—the moment we set foot on this planet, pendulums hook us.

The most common pendulum is that of your family: the people who raised you, the siblings with whom you grew up, the relationships between your family members. Together, these elements create conditions that give you an identity before you even know who you are. You behave, think, and feel in accordance with the nature of pendulums. The same goes with childhood friends and groups. Often, we can track the way we speak, our mannerisms, habits, and tendencies back to these prior relationships. From here, we develop an underlying attachment to this frequency of being, and this can be beneficial or harmful, depending on what it is, how you look at it, and how deeply you incorporate it into your being.

The three pillars that make up the pendulum of the family are mindset, behavior, and development. The process of self-discovery shines a bright light on these layers of conditioning. By contemplating who you are and how you came to be the way you are, many people discover *why* they do what they do and *how* it's led to the life they live. After self-reflection, you may find that the mindset, behavior, and development patterns in your family of origin have been holding you back from reaching your goals (or you may find that they have been fueling your success). But one thing is certain, whether we like it or not, they have an effect. Let's break each one of these pillars down.

Mindset

As noted, the family and friends with whom we grew up influence our perspective of reality. The pendulums that hooked us at an early age can be responsible for the patterns we develop throughout our lives. To break free from these patterns is not always easy. It requires that you be certain about the new direction you want to take. You must let go of your patterns, even if it means leaving the comfort of your tribe. If, for example, you grew up in a household that believed money was the root of all evil, you likely adopted limiting beliefs around being open to receiving money. If you grew up with friends who followed the rules, knelt to authority, or took a "cookie-cutter" path in life, you probably had this tendency, too. But after a long self-discovery process, you lost contact with your childhood friends, and because you chose an alternative path, you no longer resonate with those old patterns. You no longer give the pendulum that feeds that old reality your energy. Now the only thing you have in common with your childhood friend is that you came from the same place. This isn't always the case, of course, but if you have big, ambitious goals, it can be. The bigger the distance between your reality and that of your childhood friends, the bigger the disconnect.

It's important to surround yourself with people who have similar goals. Hook yourself to pendulums that pull you up. A plant can only grow as big as the pot it's in. If everyone in your circle is playing small, pivoting and engaging with a different circle of friends might help you expand your horizon. Transitioning to a new circle of friends can require careful management because some friends might challenge you, especially if your absence will disturb the energetic dynamics of the pendulum. Others will support you, sending you off with their best wishes and a "we'll keep in touch" sentiment. Others might not give your leaving much thought—and in such cases, you were not providing that pendulum much energy anyway, so it is easy to detach.

As you transition from an old pendulum to a new one, you might find yourself in a limbo phase, in which you have no friends and no new pendulum to hook on to. Do not succumb to the temptation to revert to the old pendulum. Stick to your decision. Sit in the discomfort. Instead of you being attracted to others, try creating your own pendulum to attract others to *you*. (We'll talk more about this at the end of the chapter.)

Behavior

As mentioned, pendulums can influence how you behave and interact with the world. If you aren't confident about your new path, you'll almost always bend to social norms because people without clear direction follow the tribe. It's hard-wired into our genetics. For example, if your friends go out to drink and party on the weekend, but you're trying to build healthier habits, you'll have to choose between social credit and health benefits. If you're not careful and focused, you might mimic destructive habits that lead you away from your goal. But if you surround yourself with people who focus on healthy, productive habits, it would be unnatural for you to not follow suit.

Development

The last layer of influence that pendulums have is in your personal and professional growth. When building your circle, surround yourself with people who can "add" to your life. You might think this is selfish or narcissistic, but it's not. Why can't there be a mutual, expansive exchange of value between two people? When both parties bring something to the table, whether that be physically, intellectually, energetically, or financially, it's the healthiest type of relationship. If you're enjoying giving and providing value to someone, it's because that's in alignment with your highest purpose, even if the person can't give anything back but a smile and appreciation. Give as much as you can and receive what others give you, without expectations or keeping tabs. Giving and receiving unconditionally is loving unconditionally.

A lot of relationship building is energetic. Whether or not you like to spend time around someone depends on how you feel around them. If you feel good, and they inspire you to become the best version of yourself, then so be it—if you surround yourself with people who want to grow, you'll also want to grow. To take this to the next level, imagine surrounding yourself with people who are in the position you want to be in, and who want you to be there with them. The energy exchange here is invaluable. Connecting with mentors who challenge your assumptions and expand your level of thinking could be the trigger that puts you onto an entirely new path.

When you attach yourself to pendulums that attract big thinkers and successful people, there is an element of "extra luck." Like attracts like, and when you surround yourself with people with unique knowledge, opportunities, and networks, it's only natural for you to gain value, feedback, and connections. You become a vortex for good fortune!

More often than not, money and business opportunities do not come because we pursued them. They come because we *attracted them*. So when you surround yourself with the right people, you make yourself attractive to additional levels of success. Remember, no matter where you go in this world, you'll always be under the influence of pendulums. It's important to be aware of which pendulums you're attaching yourself to because they will influence the thoughts you think, the emotions you feel, and the actions you take.

The Three Circles of Power

In the following section, we're going to look at three different circles you may need to develop for yourself, and how to optimize them to get the most out of your relationships.

Focused Manifesting

Inner Circle – Support

We all need people in our lives. We need someone whom we know has our back. Typically, that's your family. Some people find this support in a close friend. Make sure you surround yourself with people upon whom you can rely, who want the best for you, and who support you through your lowest lows and your highest highs. These are people who will tell you when you're off the rails but who will support you in taking big risks and doing something different if it's done consciously with the right intentions. These are your most vulnerable relationships, in the sense that these are people you can talk to about anything. You can share with them your biggest fears, embarrassments, or failures, and they will not judge you.

Everyone needs one friend or family member to whom they can vent. You need a place to release energy and excess potential. Holding on to your thoughts and not having anywhere to express them can lead to emotional suppression. Not everyone can play this role, so make sure you choose the right person. Journaling is a good way to articulate your thoughts too, but having someone who listens can take your expression to the next level. If you don't have this in your life right now, don't worry. Set an intention to find one or two close friends who can help.

If there is no one among your friend group or in your family or who can fill this role, consider finding a therapist or a rehab circle where you can share your thoughts in a safe environment. Having a "no judgment" zone in which to speak about your experiences (not to rant, which focuses on the negative), and reflect out loud can work wonders. Another outlet to release thoughts that might be swirling around in your head is to speak out loud when you're alone. I know this sounds "woo-woo," but having conversations with yourself can prevent you from keeping old emotions and thoughts suppressed inside you.

Online personal development communities are also good places to find these types of connections. Be diligent and patient with the people you allow into the innermost sanctum of your heart.

Mastermind Circle – Purpose

Next, you'll want to network with people who are on a similar path as you. Choose entrepreneurs, artists, leaders, or creators who have a unique mission that drives them every day. They don't need to be doing what you do (although it helps), but they should be on a journey of personal development, expansion, and mastery.

"Mastermind," a term coined by the late self-help author Napoleon Hill, relates to a group of individuals who together, with the power of collective wisdom, can propel each other to new heights and levels in all areas of life. Such a group will raise your standards, keep you accountable, and inspire you by showing you what's possible. It's true when they say that your "network is your net worth." When you surround yourself with winners, it's easy to tap into this same frequency. The more you frequent these groups, the more frequently you attract good ideas and opportunities out of thin air. These groups also offer a higher level of accountability that you won't find with people who aren't on a path to purpose and mastery.

Imagine for a second that for the first time, you attend a weekly call with your new mastermind group, and everyone shows up with updates, lessons, and wins that came from taking uncomfortable and risky action in their life or business. You, as a new member, might have nothing new or interesting to bring to the table. You'll feel out of place, like you don't belong. That's because you're not yet on the same wavelength as everyone else in the group. Instinctually, you'll take action so that next time, you'll have something to share.

Using our animal instincts to our advantage is also part of the manifestation process. We need to stop pretending we're *just* spiritual beings, because we're not. We're also human (apes with nice clothes and less hair). As you have seen, a sizeable chunk of the decisions we make result from our past conditioning and our biology. Being more spiritual and in tune with your authentic self will help you become aware of your animal instincts so that you're not a victim of them. Your body is a vehicle for living life, growing, and expanding.

Find a tribe that keeps you on your toes. Connect with a group that makes you think big. By surrounding yourself with big thinkers you will become one as well. If you feel intimidated at first, don't. You might be the newbie of the group, but you can still provide a lot of value. All it takes is for you to come into it with the right intentions and with a fresh viewpoint, which will remind others of how far they've come. Remember, everyone in your group is on the same path and they are there to support one another. So, allow them to support you as you support them in return.

Mentor Circle – Expansion

When it comes to tapping into positive pendulums, mentors can help you get there the quickest. If you find the right mentor, they will elevate you from your current reality to your desired reality, either through actions you might need to take or through giving you perspective on what you might need to shift. Having an authoritative figure to guide your decision-making and path can be a shortcut to reaching your seemingly elusive goals. If your mentor guides you correctly, they will never impose their ways on you.

Rather, they'll show you a path (or multiple paths) you can take. From there, it's your responsibility to take the necessary action, to learn the lessons you need to learn, and to recalibrate your direction as you learn new things about yourself and your endeavors.

There are many types of mentors. First, there are the life mentors, those who provide advice and direction about the path you have taken. One of my mentors, Gavin, shared countless resources he gathered along his journey that helped him develop his knowledge base and wisdom. The conversations I had with him were specific to the stage I was at in life and business. Our talks were valuable and opened me up to a new way of thinking and seeing the world.

Second, there are tactics mentors, who provide you with "step-by-step guides" that outline exact actions you need to take to achieve a specific goal. For example, a personal trainer will instruct you to do a collection of exercises based on your physiology and fitness goals. But mentors don't need to be human. For example, you could take a course about creating a YouTube channel that gives you direction on how to improve your titles, expand your reach, or keep your audience's attention. That course is your tactics mentor, providing you with specific, actionable advice. So, whether your mentor is human or digital, such strategic expertise can be helpful when you're just starting out in your journey.

When you make a personal connection with a mentor who takes you under their wing, they are inviting you to take part in their pendulum. You gain access to new frequency of energy. Being in the presence of someone who has lived the life you want to live can be a catalyst for extraordinary levels of internal shifting. For example, if you've ever attended or watched a Tony Robbins seminar, you know that the energy and enthusiasm he brings to the stage inspires workshop participants, and they leave feeling a new sense of self. Often, attendees realize quick successes after his events. My first experience with a paid mastermind (I paid upwards of $30,000) was similar. The confidence the leader, and other members had in themselves influenced me to have the same level of belief in my new offer and service. Two weeks later, I closed enough deals to pay for the entire membership fee.

A coaching client of mine, Angela, earned ten times her investment in my program after a few weeks of working together. Another client, Ashjia, made a full-time income with her trading account after a few weeks. So, as you can see, transformation and change don't need to take years to accomplish. If you surround yourself with the right people, the right thoughts and actions follow. A mixture of external guidance, the right energy pendulums, and your own intentions make this happen.

I know that we've covered a lot in this chapter, so I recommend you read it again, and let these concepts sink in. After completing the following exercises, we'll jump into thought prioritization, and deciphering the difference between thinking and focusing.

CHAPTER 5 EXERCISES

Social Circle Audit

Write down a list of all the people you interact with on a weekly basis.

Focused Manifesting

The Three Circles of Influence

Categorize each individual into one of the three circles:

- Close Circle
- Mastermind Circle
- Mentor Circle

Optimizing Circle

If you feel like you're lacking in any of the circle, answer the following questions:

a) Who or what group do you need to remove?

b) Who or what group do you need to add?

c) Where can you find the right person or community?

CHAPTER 6

THOUGHT PRIORITIZATION

Law #6:
Focus Is Creation

"Thoughts become things. If you see it in your mind, you will hold it in your hand."

Bob Proctor

This quote by the legendary self-help author and lecturer Bob Proctor makes us reflect on our thoughts: *What thoughts do I think most of the time? Where does my mind go when I'm not distracting it?* People don't manifest their dream life because of a lack of faith or effort, but because of a lack of *focus*. They have not trained themselves to calibrate their awareness according to their will. Their mind has a "mind of its own." When this happens, they get caught up in the day-to-day, reacting to one thing after another, falling victim to pendulums, and being swayed in the direction of their so-called monkey mind (or "animal mind"), that part of our mind that operates on instinct and survival.

In this chapter, we're going to looking into what it means to really *focus* and how this differentiates from what most people think it is. As we discovered in previous chapters, our thoughts aren't necessarily our own—they can arise from our childhoods and from the pendulums with which we associate. Therefore, knowing how to prioritize specific thoughts over others is a crucial step in reaching our goals.

Thinking versus Focusing

Thoughts originate in various ways. Some we generate from within us and these thoughts align with who we are and what we stand for. Others, as noted above, come from our environment and are a product of the people and distractions around us. Our minds act much like a radio. We can pick up thoughts from the quantum field. We call these unwanted thoughts that make their way to our minds *intrusive thoughts*. You can link the vast majority of these thoughts to outside forces or biological survival mechanisms.

Remember, your job is not to accept every thought that comes into your head, but to *focus on and generate the right ones.* When you know how to focus on the right things, the right thoughts come to you. Developing this skill may require self-reflection or meditation, but once you can differentiate thoughts that come *to* you from thoughts that come *from* you, you'll be better equipped to manage your focus in the face of challenges and obstacles.

Thinking is a passive process. It doesn't require much effort to think about anything. Whether you are reflecting on your past or projecting a future, your mind is processing information constantly. Thinking doesn't use free will (also known as your *power of choice*). Focus does. When you train yourself to focus, you're exercising this power of choice. This trait is *essential* to being a conscious creator of your reality.

When you're thinking mindlessly, you're not focusing. The probability that such thoughts will lead you down the right path is low. The path you go down will depend on what's stored in your subconscious mind. If you want to improve your thinking, you can't depend on the conditioning of your subconscious mind. You need to focus, and focus requires intention. Mindless thinking makes goal achievement inconsistent, because your energy is scattered and random. You are drawn to short-term pleasures and temporary highs. To change this, narrow your thinking patterns to align them with your intentions and authenticity.

Focus creates your frequency. If your focus generates thoughts, it can also influence how you feel and behave. When you change your focus, you change the signal you put out into the Universe. This shift affects not only your state of being but also *what you attract*. To practice focusing is to practice living consciously. Want to be more spiritual? Learn to focus. It's not just another productivity hack or time management tool. It's the key to living a good, fulfilling, accomplished life. If you know how to focus, you know how to create the reality you want. You know how to *manifest*.

There are two ways to maximize your ability to focus. One is through *addition*, the other is through *subtraction*. Focus through addition is about adding an element into your life that consumes your attention like a black hole. Focus through subtraction is about removing elements that serve no purpose but to steal and disperse your attention.

Blissful Obsession

Within spiritual circles, the idea of *balance* is a common topic of discussion. When it comes to our internal state of being, balance is a good thing. It is the basis of calmness, relaxation, and healing. When we're out of balance, it's because our thoughts and emotions are dragging us around like a rag doll. If you're aiming to live life with purpose and focus, balancing your inner world is crucial.

However, when we speak about the external world, the same guideline doesn't apply. When you are *doing the work* needed to achieve goals and complete projects, balance is rarely present. When you enter a phase of creation, you polarize your attention and focus on the task at hand.

Think about it. When a painter is creating a new masterpiece, they aren't checking in with their family members, scrolling through the latest news on Twitter, or distracted by sounds and people in their environment. They're focused and in flow. More often than not, they are isolated in a room or studio, laser focused on their craft and turning their vision into reality. During these moments, nothing else matters. If nothing else matters, they are unbalanced. If they are unbalanced, they are extremely focused. You manifest and create through focus, not balance.

Focused Manifesting

Herein lies one secret to focused manifesting: having a *blissful obsession.*

Our society teaches us we shouldn't obsess over anything. Obsession has a negative connotation. Often, it's associated with toxic relationships, drug addiction, or having maniacal thoughts about a certain subject or person. We're taught we shouldn't become entangled emotionally with any object of focus, because it could affect our relationships with friends and family, even our health. When you become obsessive, you add importance to your goal. This can create a sense of "not having," which, if we follow the hermetic principle of *as within, so without,* can work against you. You self-sabotage—and you can't move forward.

However, obsession doesn't need to come from a place of negativity or lack. In fact, obsession can be a good thing. It can be the fuel that lights the fire under whatever project or endeavor you embark on. When an obsession puts you in alignment with Source energy, it's called a *blissful* obsession. You don't need to suppress it. In fact, you should embrace it. By focusing on your obsession, you're aligning yourself with a purpose. Humans are purpose-driven beings. Through having a purpose (or obsession) we're better able to understand ourselves and reality, and thus, achieve fulfillment.

This is why artists that can't or don't work on their obsession become depressed. It's because they are withholding their obsession with creation. Their obsession is their fuel for living. Imagine telling a musician they can never play an instrument again. Imagine telling an athlete they can never play sports again. It's like telling a fish they can't swim. When you have something you're passionate about, whether that be making money, teaching others, doing art, or doing anything that fuels your creativity, *embrace it.* The path of your highest excitement is the path of most focus, progress, growth, and expansion.

Seek Harmony

Achieving any goal requires an unbalanced approach for a temporary period. By having an overarching goal that you prioritize, you funnel your attention and energy. When you do this, you can manifest a reality at much quicker and more efficient rate.

Nowadays, online creators call this short period of hyper-focus toward a singular goal (or your Chief Aim) *Monk Mode*. It's about establishing a period between one to six months to focus most of your attention on completing a project or building the foundation of a business. For example, maybe you set out to write a book in ninety days. This is not an impossible goal. However, I'd say that ninety percent of people who think about writing a book never do. If they start, they don't finish. If they finish, they never publish. If they publish, it doesn't sell. This made me wonder, *What's missing from the ninety percent's strategy?*

In 2021, for about eight months, I was the head coach for the biggest online self-publishing education platform in the world. It was a good, part-time gig that taught me a lot about the online education space and consulting. During one of our meetings, the founder showed us the clients' journey from the moment they joined the course to the moment they submitted their final action items. Less than five percent of thousands of students reached the end of the program, let alone published their first book. I wondered, *Why does this happen? Why do people pay for education and never apply it? Did they lack focus?*

If you're not excited enough about publishing a book, running a business, or making an impact, then there's only a slight chance

Focused Manifesting

you'll take action on it. The people who act on information they have gained recently are obsessed. They envelope their world with the insights they've gleaned and apply them with *speed* and *a sense of curiosity*—and they always expect that it will work out or that they will learn something new.

People who accomplish nothing big or significant aren't obsessed. They're okay with living the life they have now, and there's nothing wrong with that. It takes a certain level of intrinsic motivation to move you into action. This is why, in Chapter 1, we worked on picking goals that are both exciting and believable. If you pick a goal that isn't exciting for you, or isn't believable, chances are slim that you'll take any action on it.

Be okay with being obsessed and out of balance for a bit. Be okay with prioritizing one thing and maintaining just a few others. Focus on your calling. Move with the flow of your intuition. Be purpose-driven. Do not allow external expectations and judgments stop you from fulfilling the calling in your heart. Be okay with being an outlier or looking crazy. Everyone thought I was weird when I spent eighteen months locked in my parents' house writing books about personal development and spirituality. Now they ask me how I did it.

It takes being a little "out there" to create a life that's not normal. If all you do is follow the norms and rules of society, you'll create the life most people live. Ask anybody walking down the street if they're even eighty percent satisfied with their life. Most people will say "No" because they're not following their authentic calling. If they were, others would call them maniacal, crazy, or *obsessed*. But really, they are not happy because they are not living in harmony with their soul's purpose.

We define harmony as, "*A relationship in which various components exist together without destroying one another.*" In short, by living in harmony and prioritizing, we're able to leverage our input to maximize our output. When we give something energy, it grows. When we funnel most of our energy to it, it flourishes.

On top of this, harmony allows you to overcome and look past the struggles and challenges that are bound to come along your journey. If your intentions are weak, the first sign of difficulty will set you off course. When you're more connected with the process than you are with the results, doing what's necessary to stay on track is natural.

Be in perfect flow with the Universe, and in perfect flow with your intuition and highest excitement. This is how you'll be able to give your all to something without losing yourself. You're not making this decision with your mind or rationality. You're making it based on divine guidance. A blissful obsession with a mission, purpose, or goal is like a line of code for your soul. It's part of your internal design. Do not allow society to stop you from giving your attention to that which is driven by Source energy.

Live in the extremes. Tackle short-term goals and endeavors with sprints while knowing the game is a marathon. Accomplishing little things and completing projects here and there, stacked over a long enough period, is all there is to it. Forget about results for now. By taking the right steps forward, the results come. Allow yourself to fall in love with a process. Any process. This is the path of less "wanting" and more "having."

The Non-Importance of Practically Everything

Separating *what's important to us* with *what's not important to us* is our job alone. Once we realize this, we also realize the unimportance of everything. The only reason we give importance to most things is because other people give them importance. To find your focus, define what is *essential* in your life. Narrow the pillars of reality you want to prioritize. It's like the Buddha said, "Desire is the root of all suffering." If you have too many desires, you're going to put yourself into a box of misery and struggle. When you define what's important to you, you make yourself less vulnerable to the movements and changes of the external world.

The world is changing fast. If you care too much about all the changes in government, geo-politics, technology, the stock market, etc., you're opening yourself up to a world of pain. By defining the few things that are important to you, you remain neutral to the millions and trillions of pendulums that are trying to steal your attention and energy. When you do this, the steps you need to take become clear and simple.

The purpose of this sub-section is to get clear about your inner compass. *What factors drive your decision-making? What are the pillars of your dream reality?* Once you identify these, it's easier to set your values and boundaries, creating a clear path in the direction you want to go. If you don't have a clear-cut path, all it takes is one flashy news headline to change your state of being for the rest of the day—and even the direction you intend to take. By defining what's important, you protect yourself energetically.

Here are two mindset shifts you can start to embrace:

1. Say "No" more often.

    Once you've defined what you want to prioritize, start saying "No" to things that aren't in alignment with your core pillars. In the beginning, this can be uncomfortable because we've conditioned ourselves to say "Yes" in order to please those around us. If following your heart and setting these boundaries affects the way a relationship unfolds, it most likely would not last, anyway. When you prioritize your alignment with the pillars of your dream reality, you're prioritizing manifesting that reality.

2. The "I choose to" mindset.

It's easy to fall into the "I need to" trap. Often, you have responsibilities that require your attention and energy. However, don't label them as something you *need* to do, because it implies that you have no say. With time, the more you let go and align with your pillars, the less you're going to feel you need to do anything. Every "problem" begins to align with your priorities. Therefore, everything that shows up is just another event helping you align with the path you've chosen. *Problems become opportunities when they come from your priorities.* This differentiates good problems from bad problems.

For example, say you want to prioritize your business for the next twelve months. However, every night, you get into a fight with your spouse. These fights are bad problems because they take energy away from your priority. Now, imagine your business is in a slump, with low sales. Because this new problem aligns with your priority, it's a good problem to have because it's an opportunity for you to improve your product and your marketing and sales strategies, etc.

One way to organize your life pillars to create harmony between them is to use the Eisenhower Decision Matrix, as shown below.

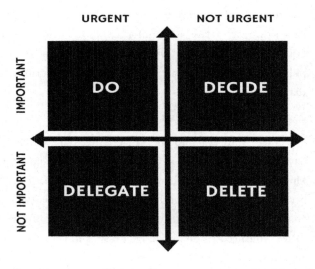

Sometimes one pillar requires more urgency than the others. Say, for example, this pillar is your health. For the next season in your life, this pillar would take priority. You'd focus on being more consistent with the gym and regulating what you eat. You would maintain everything else or put it on the back-burner. *Urgency* is the metric that defines which life pillars are worth honing in on temporarily. In fact, urgency can influence your Chief Aim, and the maintenance and back-burner goals discussed in Chapter 1.

When I'm in flow while working, rarely do I allow anything or anyone to steal that moment from me. However, if someone came knocking on my door telling me a close friend or family member needs me, I wouldn't hesitate. One of the most effective ways to live a life with more harmony is to set your course, but then be flexible when navigating it. You never know where the wind will blow, but you can always be ready to adjust the sails. Establish boundaries to gain focus without allowing them to hinder your adaptability.

Once you've established boundaries around what you give your attention to, you can shift tasks without losing focus. See how this works? When you focus on your prioritizes, you only allow your priorities to distract you. This makes focus feel effortless. You can have ADHD and be the most scattered, disorganized person on the planet, but if the only thing that can steal your attention are life pillars that align with your end goal, you're always going to be on the right path.

Manifestation runs on the Universe's clock. If we want to focus and manifest quicker, bigger results, we need to align with *divine timing*. Everything we've talked about in this book is to put you in alignment with the current season of your life, so you can pursue short-term goals that are believable for you *now*, that you're obsessed about *now*, that demand a certain level of urgency *now*, and that help you grow quicker into the person you need to become *now*. When you're present with the process, every step you take is the right one.

By following divine timing, it becomes easier to get into the flow of the constant movement, changes, and fluctuations of reality. Focus does not have to be about being rigid, stubborn, or trapped. It can be fluid, if you know how to set up your environment, define your values, and then be adaptable with your approach.

In the next chapter, we'll look at how your emotions play a role in developing your focus. Given the years of conditioning we all have, fluctuations and changes in life plans aren't easy to manage emotionally. Once you know how to manage the emotional layer of your reality, you no longer need to work on your dreams, because they work for *you*.

CHAPTER 6 EXERCISES

Defining Obsession

What are you blissfully obsessed about? If you don't have any, what would you like to build a blissful obsesses with?

Pillars of Reality

a) What are your life values? Write down a list of as many as you can.

b) Pick a top 5. These are your life pillars.

Reducing Importance

Where are you placing an excess amount of importance?

Focused Manifesting

Creating Harmony

What areas of your life could you potentially give less attention to, in order to focus more on your blissful obsession?

CHAPTER 7

EMOTIONAL DISTRACTIONS

Law #7: Emotions Are Mechanical and Impersonal

"Distraction is the only thing that consoles us for miseries and yet it is itself the greatest of our miseries."

Blaise Pascal

We human beings are emotional creatures. Emotions give flavor to our lives. Without emotions, we'd be like robots running on code, leaving no room for spontaneity, inspiration, or divine intelligence to come into play. Emotions play an important role in our development. They can be a useful guidance system and can uplift our mundane day-to-day routine. However, emotions are tricky in that most people don't know how to handle them when they come. Your emotions can serve as a tool for growth or they can be a distraction that puts your growth on hold. You can be a victim to your emotions or you can use them to your advantage.

By remaining non-attached to your emotions, you're better able to use them for the mechanism that they are—and improve your life. You may feel sad, angry, or happy, but none of these emotions define who you are at your core. Process your emotions. Work with them, but do not think they are *you*. When we approach our emotional world this way, we're viewing it from a higher perspective.

Emotions are mechanical. They're not random. When it comes to what emotions you feel and when you feel them, *cause* and *effect* is at play. In this chapter, we'll go over the mechanics of emotions and how to engage with them so you can use them to improve your life, rather than have them be an insistent distraction pulling you away from your primary focus.

Your Personal Guidance System

In simple terms, emotions are *energy in motion*. This energy is an outward expression of an inner belief you have when you face a particular situation or event. When your beliefs aren't in alignment with your true essence, you feel negative emotions. When they are, you feel positive ones.

Your emotions are a guidance system. When you feel a negative emotion, it is a clear indicator you are holding a belief you need to shift. For example, if you experience a lot of anger, you're likely holding an old, hidden belief of lack, scarcity, or insecurity. The time it will take to dissolve these beliefs will depend on how long this emotional imprint has been there and how deep it is.

Your mind bookmarks your memories with emotions. A specific emotional state becomes a snapshot of the past. That's why you always have a specific *feeling* whenever you're remembering a past moment. Your emotions anchor your memories, and your mind associates past events or traumas with those emotions. The byproduct of emotional memories is that we become convinced that a false narrative we hold about ourselves is true.

Now, this is where people get confused. When we're on a path, focusing on our goals, negative emotions will sometimes be part of our experience. Stepping into the unknown and doing something new always leads to a bit of fear and self-doubt. This does *not* mean that the path you're on is not for you. It does, however, mean that the new perspective you are developing to sustain your new reality hasn't yet grown into a belief that's affected your emotions. Your older belief is still dominant. This is why, when you try new things or face something unexpected, it's uncomfortable. Negative emotions surface. It's normal. *Emotions should gauge your perspectives and beliefs, not define them.*

The key is to immerse yourself in this new reality. If you face a challenge 100 times over, it will no longer be uncomfortable. It will be a part of your *identity*. Hence, you'll no longer feel the emotional turmoil that once came from experiencing that challenge. When you change your perspective, and sit consistently with the emotion it brings, you step into a new way of being. The biggest mistake people make is they avoid this process because it's uncomfortable. As a result, they allow old emotions to run their lives. This is when the body commands the mind, and not the other way around.

We can't allow our emotions to distract us from our path. Instead, we need to use them as guides to help us navigate our path. Many people fall victim to their emotions. They avoid doing what's *necessary* and instead do what's *comfortable*. When you follow this route, you're bound to live an unfulfilling life sprinkled with a sense of lack and low confidence.

You can't develop confidence, patience, or resilience by doing what you've always done. Confidence comes from competence. To be competent, you need to be patient with the learning process. To develop patience, you need to be resilient to all the obstacles, challenges, and setbacks that come your way. The traits we all desire can only come from experiencing the trials and tribulations that help us develop them.

In order to gain mastery over the emotional body, you must understand a few principles:

- *It's not logical:* The body communicates to the mind through the emotions. When the body faces situations that remind it of past traumatic events or when it's defending an identity, it will project the same emotional state as a means of informing the mind.

- When this happens, *catch yourself in the emotion*: This way, you use the emotional state as a *mental anchor* to travel back to the memory and heal or reinterpret the event, correcting the flow of energy in your life.

- *Don't resist emotions:* We often make the mistake of trying to internalize our emotions. We teach men not to cry, and this raises the question: *Is this why men have a higher rate of heart attacks than women do?* When you suppress emotions, you give them the power to surface when you least expect them. The key to managing your emotions is to not resist them. Allow them to be. Observe them without judgment. Letting go of your emotions is a crucial step in reducing one of life's biggest distractions— the emotionally conditioned body.

Emotion and Intuition

While emotions and intuition are related, it's common for people to confuse them. Here's the common misconception: if you feel bad, you're on the wrong path, and when you feel good, you're on the right path. This couldn't be further from the truth. When you know how to differentiate emotions and intuition, you'll understand your body's signals and how to use them to your advantage.

As Law #7 states, emotions are mechanical and impersonal. Emotions result from conditioning based on life experiences and the meanings the mind gives to these experiences. Intuition taps into a deeper sense of knowing beyond logical reasoning. It's the whispers of the soul and of your higher self. Intuition goes beyond what we're able to understand. How do you know which is which? The shortest answer? *Awareness.*

Emotions feel right; intuition is right.

In making decisions, most people follow their emotions. However, their emotions are often a collection of past and future stories. This does not mean they are true. With decision-making, reflect on whether you're "traveling in time" when deciding.

For example, say you bought an online course once, and you didn't enjoy the product. Many people, having had this experience, might fall into the trap of believing that *all* online courses are scams. Emotions are irrational, so they lead us to generalizing and overreacting. In this situation, a person will likely hold back on buying another online training course, even if there was the high probability of it providing immense amounts of value.

Often, we make decisions hoping to avoid repeating an experience or we are fantasizing about a future we want to experience. This backward-looking and forward-imagining clouds your decisions, which makes them less likely to be right. Does this mean we should never consider past or future? Of course not. However, do not fall victim to your own biases and limited self-experiences.

If you're going to play the game of life at the highest level, you need to train your intuition and become familiar with the subtle ways it speaks to you. Many of the world's most successful entrepreneurs credit intuition as their guiding light.

"In the same way that I tend to make up my mind about people within thirty seconds of meeting them, I also make up my mind about whether a business proposal excites me within about thirty seconds of looking at it. I rely far more on gut instinct than researching huge amounts of statistics."

Richard Branson

Your intuition is a whisper. It's difficult to pinpoint intuition because it's not a feeling. It's an inner knowing. There is no bodily sensation, chemical release, or rational thought process. When you decide something based on your intuition, you take a leap of faith. In the beginning, your mind and emotions could make you feel like you've made the wrong decision, but intuition will always guide you toward highest service to yourself and the collective in the long run. It's the path of most fulfillment because you're following your inner truth.

The bigger the decision, the louder your emotions and intuition will be. Your emotions will "make the most noise," so be aware of this. Despite the effectiveness of our intuition, there's nothing wrong with checking in with your thoughts and emotions first. Consider the variables at play. Sometimes, putting your intuition on hold can be the best course of action. For example, your intuition might be telling you to quit your job, but if you have kids to take care of and bills to pay, nicking away at transitioning from your job little by little will make more sense. If left unchecked, emotions can be a big distraction. They might sidetrack you and keep you from listening to your intuition and staying focused on your purpose. Luckily, there is a simple technique for managing emotional distress when you're trying to stay focused.

Surfing the Urge

I do not recommend forcing your way through emotional distress. There are many other better alternatives. Using sheer willpower to tackle challenging situations will lead to frustration, guilt, and a sense of powerlessness. Again, what you resist persists. The better way to manage your emotional distractions is to *negotiate* with them. For example, say you're at work and a task gets difficult. Regardless of the task, time of day, or your energy level, you shift to something that's easier to do—for example, maybe you pick up your phone and scroll through social media.

The pendulum of the phone drains you of your energy and you lose your momentum. You are no longer producing work of

Focused Manifesting

a high quality. This repeats, and a two-hour task turns into a six-hour one. A one-week project becomes a one-month project. When you're distracted, you slow down your production time and lower the standard of your output. Here are two solutions:

1. Notice when you get distracted. What's the common theme?

2. Surf your emotional urge for five to ten minutes before acting on it.

By sitting with your emotion for a while, you'll be better able to evaluate its strength and source. The key is to *surf the urge*. Instead of trying to fight your emotion, be patient. Instead of trying to avoid your urges, cravings, and impulses, sit with them. Give yourself five to ten minutes to listen to the emotion. Before you know it, the emotion will dissipate, and you'll be back into your workflow. You can see this being reflected in ancient Japanese practices, like in the *Pomodoro Technique*, where you work for twenty-five minutes and rest for five minutes. The five minutes allows your mind and emotions to settle before continuing on with work.

Going to the bathroom, juggling oranges, taking a walk, or just sitting in silence are all effective ways of surfing an urge without succumbing to it. When you get back to work, you're refreshed because you didn't spend that time giving your energy away to a distraction. If your urge is still there after ten minutes, indulge in it. This is part of the negotiation. Keep to your promise. However, you'll find that nine out of ten times, the "need" to indulge diminishes during your ten minutes of downtime. Your tendency will be to refocus to your task with a new set of insights. This is an effective way to change any habit, regardless to what it pertains to. You don't need to force and punish yourself. Let the dust settle, and your vision will be clear.

Spiritual Dopamine

Until this point, we've talked about how your emotions can be a major distraction. Another layer to this is *emotional dependency*. This is when someone depends on a certain emotion to take a certain course of action. We wait until we are happy to tell someone we love them. We wait until something stresses us before we start getting our life together. We wait to start a business until we feel motivated. We spend too much time waiting to feel something before we take action on the things we want to do.

There are days we feel unmotivated and misaligned. A bad night of sleep, lack of clarity, or stress can all be factors. When the effort required to do something you have to do doesn't seem worth the reward, you can feel unmotivated. It tests your discipline. In these moments, your motivation is to *not* do what you know you need to do. Fortunately, there is a way to draw motivation from within, and maintain the focus required to grow in any area of life. I call this producing *spiritual dopamine*. But before we jump into an explanation of that term, let's inspect what dopamine is.

Dopamine is the "pleasure molecule." It's the "reward" our brain gives us for engaging in a pleasurable activity. This is an addictive chemical that gets people *hooked*. Whether the activity we engage in is beneficial for us or not is irrelevant. You can get dopamine from completing meaningful work, just like you can get dopamine from scrolling on social media or from eating chocolate.

You can alter your dopamine levels to train your attention and enhance your spiritual practices, thereby aligning with your goals and dreams. It's common practice to do ten-day meditation retreats to *starve* the brain of dopamine. When you get back from the retreat, everything (even work you once thought was boring)

Focused Manifesting

seems stimulating. This is when being aligned with your purpose feels good both to the brain AND the heart. So how does it work?

The reason we struggle with using dopamine to our advantage is because in our society, we've become desensitized to it. We engage too often in activities that result in overloading ourselves with dopamine, like eating sugary foods, scrolling through social media, checking emails, playing video games, etc. When we engage in meaningless activities that produce more dopamine than the meaningful work produces, the mind resists focusing on the latter. But there is a way to make "boring" or "difficult" work a primary source of pleasure. The key? Recalibrate your neurological reward system to align it with your spiritual essence. Here's how you can do this:

1) Practice doing nothing.

This might seem paradoxical, but one of the simplest ways to improve your focus is by learning how to focus on *nothing*. When taking breaks from work, waiting in line, or taking an Uber, our immediate reaction is to pick up the phone, keeping dopamine production "ON."

The key with this technique is to turn your dopamine production "OFF," just as you would if you were in a meditation retreat. You don't need to spend thousands of dollars traveling to a temple in a third-world country to do this. Get good at watching the water pass through your coffee filter, staring at a plant, sitting in silence, or taking a walk (without headphones). Train yourself to be bored. This is when "the work" becomes "the fun."

2) Do one thing at a time.

The less you give your attention to, the easier it is to produce meaningful dopamine. By creating a funnel for your awareness, you're facilitating access to higher states of consciousness. So, when you're eating, just eat. When you're working, just work. When you're talking with people, just talk. Multi-tasking will only spread your attention and reduce your ability to *be* who you want to be at every moment.

In this chapter, we've discussed ways of managing emotions that hinder our focus and cause inner turmoil. Managing your emotions requires more *unlearning* than it does *learning*. It requires letting go of a familiar feeling and stepping into one you aren't used to. Remember, emotions drive us human beings. Once you've shifted, everything else flows with ease.

CHAPTER 7 EXERCISES

Defining Emotional Distractions

What emotions and urges are distracting you from staying focused? These are the ones that come up when things get difficult, uncomfortable, or boring.

Defining Escapes

When you feel these emotions, what behaviors do you tend to carry out? What are the distraction you gravitate towards? Write down a list of them below.

Alternative Escapes

Instead of engaging in the behaviors previously listed, what are some alternative behaviors you can do to surf the urge? Write down a list of them below.

CHAPTER 8

MENTAL STORIES OF SELF

Law #8: Your Story Is Malleable

"The timeless in you is aware of life's timelessness, And knows that yesterday is but today's memory and tomorrow is today's dream."

Khalil Gibran, The Prophet

If we were to audit the thoughts of one million people on a second-to-second basis, we'd realize that a lot of their attention is going *inwards*. They are listening to their own thoughts. Creating narratives. Speaking to themselves. Coming up with answers for the past or plans for the future. Most people spread their imaginations across a spectrum of pasts and futures. They time travel.

Time is mental—it's how we're able to track motion through space. Time is also relative—it's not the same for everyone. For example, people serving prison sentences experience time at a slower pace than kids during recess. However, in society we accept "time" as a fixed reality. We live by the clock, by the records we keep, by the memories we have of the past, or by our projections of the future. However, if you think about it, most clocks are not in sync with "real time" (which in the U.S.A. is the NIST-F1 Cesium Fountain Atomic Clock, at the National Institute of Standards and Technology in Boulder, Colorado). Most records are an account of a past experienced from the perspective of the person who wrote the record. There are many gaps in history, filled with untold and mis told stories. Most memories are clouded with bias and emotions. Nobody experiences time the same way. Time, as they say, is an illusion.

So what's the purpose of time? By keeping time, we maintain an arbitrary measuring system by which we can dictate people's actions, interpret their accomplishments, and track their advances through space. With this system in place, people can get organized, communicate effectively, and, if they are synced with one another, they can achieve great things. However, even though our society runs on time, it's important to understand that *time is not real*.

The memories you have about your past are not the past, but are instead images and ideas you hold in the *present*. When you look back at a memory, you're not traveling to the past and reliving the experience. Your brain simulates the past based on what it *thinks* happened, and this is determined by how you think *now*. *Your current thoughts create your past and future.*

The subconscious mind does not understand the difference between a *genuine* experience and an *imagined* one. For the subconscious, whatever you conjure isn't just a memory or a future projection, it's an actual event happening right now. With your conscious mind, you can add context to your thoughts and place them within a particular time period, but the subconscious is timeless. It exists in the now. It lives in the present. As you think your thoughts and tell yourself your stories, you live and experience them in the *now*.

This mechanism of time can come into play to distract you. Imagine you're giving a presentation at work, and your mind conjures up a time when someone bullied you as a kid. If you haven't processed that memory, it'll throw you off track. Your palms will sweat. You'll stumble on your words. You'll lose your edge. Even though you know this image in your mind is an illusion, the emotions and pressure the memory conjures will make you react emotionally and physically, as though the bullying is happening right now.

Who you are is who you choose to be right now. When other people tell you about your past, they're projecting the story that's going on inside their head. When you realize all you have is right now, no imaginary past or future should ever come between you and who you choose to be.

Another side to memories is that they are not *fixed*. What you remember of your past is *not* what happened. For example, think of one of your earliest memories. Notice how the memory is fragmented—there are only a few blips and highlights. The longer we go without thinking about a memory, the less reliable it becomes. The less emotionally attached we are to an event, the less likely we are to remember it. When we look back at a memory, it's been distorted and reinterpreted so many times, you can't say with certainty what happened. Not only that, it's only your perspective. Other people might have had a different perspective. *Never confuse memory with reality.*

If all of your memories are subjective, then all of your past is a story you tell yourself. It's the story of your life. The story you *choose* to believe. If you change the story, you change your self. If you change your belief, you change your identity. *You are who you say you are.*

The more I've solo traveled, the more I've realized that we can be whomever we want to be. When nobody knows who you are, you can rewrite your story. You can live a different life than the one you think you're supposed to live. We all have control over the stories we tell ourselves (and others). When you change your timeline and story, you change the frequency of your being and reality. This changes the way you focus, which changes the way you think and act, which changes the things you create and attract. Therefore, by knowing how to change your stories, you can have a significant effect on your ability to manifest. The challenge is knowing how and when to do this. Later on in this chapter, we'll be discussing three different techniques. You are the author of your story. But before you can write timelessly, you need to *become timeless.*

Becoming Timeless

Virtually every spiritual teaching alludes to the idea of eternity, of oneness with the Universe. Whether it's the Big Bang Theory, or the story of Creation, every object of focus is a unique expression of the

Focused Manifesting

same one consciousness. We are all connected, and in fact, we are the same thing expressing itself in different ways. In Hermetic teachings, *you are a fractal of The All in which all exists for infinity.* Once we recognize this, we tap into our timeless nature. This is one of the main purposes of meditation—to reconnect with timelessness. Before you can shift who you are, you must become nobody at all. From this point on, you can choose your new story or the new identity you want to embody. *For a cup to be filled, first you must empty it.*

This is easier said than done. Your ego is the creator of all your mental stories. It exists only in your mind, and when your mind becomes *no-thing*, the ego ceases to exist. So the ego wants us to jump from one thought to the next in order to avoid the stillness. Why? Because in the stillness there is no one, no body, no thing, in *no time*, and in this space, there is no ego.

To keep our minds busy and active (in time), we seek distractions, which stop us from reconnecting with Source. When we're distracting ourselves, we become victims to the mental stories and narratives our egos create. We become victims to the stories others have conditioned us to believe rather than the stories we ourselves have created.

When you meditate, aim to listen to the sound of silence. Look back at the darkness and emptiness. Seek the clarity that comes from being aware of awareness. When you realize you are the *observer* of your mind, you recognize that which doesn't change, that which is timeless. We know this as *the transition point*, the point at which you stop telling yourself one story after another, and you just are.

To change your story, you need to change the illusion of time. To do this, first you must recognize it is an illusion. When you change your story, you're changing the focal point of your identity. When this happens, focusing on the right thoughts feels effortless. You take action not because you think you should, but because it's *who you are*. As you sink into the silence, the space between your thoughts widens. Within this space you discover nothingness. We know how to do this when we go to sleep. The only difference is that we allow ourselves to go unconscious before we give ourselves enough time to sit in the nothingness. At the moment right before you fall asleep, your brain is in an alpha-wave state. This is a state of complete surrender and relaxation: the transition point.

When you're meditating, do as you would if you were falling asleep, but don't fall asleep. Keep your mind conscious and aware. (I don't recommend meditating lying down because it is too easy to fall asleep. The best position for meditation is to find somewhere comfortable enough for you to sit up straight and relaxed for an extended period.) Surrendering your mind to nothingness is a revealing process. It will teach you about your thoughts and where your attention goes. It will show you which emotions are linked with which thoughts, and how dominant they both are in your day-to-day life. Hindu sage Ramana Maharshi calls this process *self-inquiry*. It's about placing your attention back to the awareness of "I" or "I am." The sooner you recognize and become familiar with this awareness, the easier it will be to adapt to new ways of being in alignment with your goals. Manifestation then becomes about letting go of the stories holding you back rather than doing what you think you need to do.

This is a powerful practice for those who feel themselves to be victims of their own self-proclaimed identity. "I can't because I am XYZ," or "I won't because I am XYZ." When you realize that who you are originates from something much deeper, you're better

Focused Manifesting

able to accept the possibility of having a state and identity that's fluid and adaptable. You don't need to force yourself to develop the skill to focus. Focus should result from an internal change in your identity.

When you work with your thoughts and emotions in this way, you can uncover the roots of your stories. By recognizing these stories, and realizing your identity and who you truly are, you're better able to pinpoint where you need to shift. We create reality based on the view we have of both the world and ourselves. When you change your story and the story you tell others, you change your reality. Here's how to do it....

Shift the Past to Recreate the Present

When you practice the technique of shifting the past, here are some golden rules to remember...

- The only moment in time that exists is *here and now*.

- Your story is only as malleable as you believe it to be.

- Changing your story requires letting go and having faith.

- Always remember, you are more than just your thoughts and memories.

- The new story must be believable to a certain extent. You're not writing a fantasy novel.

- Be authentic and genuine with the story you choose to embody.

Understand this: *Anybody* can do this kind of work. It doesn't matter how scarred you believe yourself to be, you can change the look, perspective, and meaning of those scars to fit a new, empowering narrative. As long as you can use your imagination, this will work. There are three different techniques to this work:

- *redefining,*

- *eliminating,* and

- *rewriting.*

Begin with the parts of your story that distract you, the ones that pull you out of becoming who you're meant to be or that make you feel fearful, insecure, and/or limited.

Once you've defined these parts, choose the techniques that are easiest to apply, but that also give you the most confidence and make you feel like your authentic self. Choose one or a combination of all three techniques to change and empower this new version of your story. Let's start with *redefining.*

Redefine

This technique focuses on the parts of your story you define as "negative," "detrimental," and/or "the reason you're not where you want to be." These parts are anchors. They are the events "stopping you" from reaching the next stage in your development. They are events you blame and point your finger at the most. Once you've defined them, it's time to flip the narrative on its head. When we see a past event from a negative perspective, we're creating an excuse not to embody the traits we want. This excuse is a cushion for the ego. When you have the potential to change and evolve, the ego uses this part of your story to avoid shifting and stepping into the unknown. When you notice this happening, it's time to change the timeline of the event.

Begin by accepting all the potential negatives that came from this event. Shine a light on all your blame. This might lead to a sense of unworthiness, guilt, shame, or anger. Do not suppress these emotions. Feel into them. Surf the urge. Acknowledge them as they come. Once you've acknowledged them, accept them. Let go. You are not the thought that led to the emotions, nor are you the emotions themselves. Process them and release the energy you've been giving to them.

Next, highlight all the positives that have happened because of this event. In what way did it shift your direction in life? Whom did you meet? What did you accomplish? What lessons did you learn? How did all this speed up your growth? By flooding your mind with alternative perspectives, you see the positive in every event.

The only reason we hold on to one perspective is because we didn't consider the possibility of redefining it. The emotional imprint it created led to a chain of thoughts, narratives, and beliefs that keep you stuck with a tunnel-vision view of the event. By redefining its effects, you're changing the timeline you're on. The event is no longer limiting you. Instead, it is empowering you to step into your greatness. Remember, you are no longer the participant, but a mere observer of the memory. This concept is best explained with the story of the twin brothers.

One day, two twin brothers were born. They were raised in a middle-class family. Their mother was a homemaker, their father was a lawyer who struggled with alcoholism. This led to many dark nights at their house, leading to the dismantlement of the family. The parents got divorced, the father continued to abuse his authority, and all the while the brothers were caught in the middle.

As they grew older, one of the twin brothers became a successful business executive. The other turned into an alcoholic like his father. A news reporter interviewed the two brothers to get a grasp of what had happened. Why did one brother become successful while the other fell into the same trap as his father? When asked, both brothers gave the same reply, "How could I not? My father was an alcoholic."

People can experience the same event, but take away different lessons. When a past event is not mentally or emotionally supporting your development, it's worth reflecting on it, and redefining what it meant to go through what you went through. By doing this, you open yourself up to an entire new realm of possibility. You write a new story.

Depending on how intense your memories are, you might have to take it slow with this exercise. Looking back at these memories can sometime trigger emotional overwhelm or pain you've refused to feel for a long time. This is okay. Take your time with it and understand that the more you expose yourself to these stories, the easier it'll be to shift them.

Eliminate

Have you ever met someone who is living a different life now than the life they lived in the past? Maybe they live in a new city, or they got a new job, made new friends, changed their personality or their lifestyle, or are even speaking a new language? To make that happen, they detached themselves from their past. This next technique eliminates any association you have with specific periods of your past. You are, in a phrase, emptying your cup.

Even if your story didn't scar you mentally, emotionally, or physically, it still plays a big role in how you define yourself, and it still takes up unnecessary bandwidth. Themes such as what schools you went to, the culture you grew up in, or the places you've worked can all be a part of your story that doesn't *add* to the new story or identity you want to embody. Redefining yourself can help you shrug off that old story, but a quicker route to reducing the attention you give to your old story is to eliminate it. We already do this with events we're not attached to emotionally. For example, few people remember what they had for dinner last week because it's not important. You can do the same with stories you give importance to but don't have emotional bonds with.

Of course, this is easier when you're starting fresh in a new city or country; making travel another powerful tool for focus shifting. Wherever and whenever you "start from scratch," your story can be whatever you want it to be. It can start and end as you wish. You can even separate it into two different stories if you'd like: e.g. "... before I moved to XYZ, and after I moved to XYZ." Creating this separation opens space in your mind to only think about one point and beyond. The rest doesn't have a bearing in your life. Here are a few ways you can create a separation:

1. Create a ritual to symbolize the end of a story. For example, writing an open-hearted letter about the period, pouring out all of your feelings, and then burning it.

2. Reduce the importance you give to that period in your life. If you don't want it to have a say, it shouldn't matter anymore. Dissociate with everything it involves. There are two simple ways to do this: (a) accept all possibilities that could come from the story, and (b) have a Plan-B for worst-case scenarios.

3. Split your story into multiple chapters. By segmenting your story, you give your mind direction. Which chapter

do you want to focus on and give your attention to? Big life changes (like moving to another city) facilitate the creation of these chapters.

Not every memory needs to take up space in your mind. If it's not that important, eliminating it can open up mental bandwidth so you can give new possibilities the attention they deserve.

Rewrite

Think back to a time you had a unique experience with a friend, and you heard them tell the story to others. Depending on the friend, the story may seem less interesting than your version of it. Or they might over-exaggerate it and even add elements you didn't realize were there. Maybe they make that past, shared event feel like something *less* or *more* than it was, adding or removing details or emotions, or suggesting you felt something that you don't remember feeling.

Is this lying? Not necessarily. It's overemphasizing or under-emphasizing the moment depending on how relevant it is to the timeline (the series of events that make up the story of your life) you want to be on. I learned this from speaking with Brazilians. They are excellent story tellers. They will turn a normal life event into a memory you end up telling everyone about.

An example can be of you overemphasizing moments of "timid confidence," moments in which you might not have felt super confident but took a risk anyway and it worked out. Here, there's no shame in embracing the idea that you felt confident. Do not undermine your accomplishments, especially the internal ones. Be proud. *Own your successes.*

When it comes to under-emphasizing, you may already do this when you're telling a story about something embarrassing.

But what if you didn't limit it to just these moments? Under-emphasizing moments you give too much importance to can help you and others forget the event even happened. Removing emotions removes the memory. This is a powerful technique. Do not go too crazy with your "mental edits," but make enough of them so that the present you can own and relay your rewritten stories to others with confidence and authenticity.

Do not be the victim of your story. Be its author. Awareness is your pen, imagination is your ink, and your mind is the canvas. Do what you have to do to create an empowering story that fuels your creativity and reassures you as you walk your chosen path.

CHAPTER 8 EXERCISES

Writing Your New Story

Write down your new story from beginning to end in 7-10 chapters. Give a name or year to each chapter, and describe each in a few sentences.

- Remember to incorporate the following principles:
- This is your hero's journey - you're the protagonist.
- Redefine breakdowns as breakthroughs.
- Eliminate what's irrelevant to you and has no more room.
- Rewrite to add more emphasis. Make your story epic.

Focused Manifesting

CHAPTER

9

NARROWING ATTENTION

Law #9: The Essential Few Trumps the Trivial Many

"Things that matter most must never be at the mercy of things that matter least."

Richard Koch

Focused Manifesting

In a world abundant with opportunities, it's difficult to *not* be doing something, being somewhere, or seeing someone. Nowadays, the most common reply to a "How's life?" question seems to be "Busy!" Having free time has become synonymous with being of inferior status, because in our world, we glorify being occupied and unavailable.

When I first began my journey into entrepreneurship, money wasn't my main focal point. Of course, it was a necessary and important component, but the real driver? *Freedom*. I wanted the freedom to say "Yes" to taking a spontaneous trip. The freedom to live anywhere in the world. The freedom to start work at 1:30 p.m. The freedom to choose what I want to create next. The freedom to disconnect for thirty days if I want to do so.

Now that I've manifested my freedom, I've reflected on the core principles that have helped me. They all revolve around the idea of *narrowing my attention*. As author, podcaster, and former Navy Seal Jocko Willink says, discipline equals freedom. Too many of us... spend a lot of time... trying to accomplish a lot of things... all at once.

Energy is a *finite* resource. Therefore, if you are not funneling it into the right goals, actions, and tasks, you're spreading yourself thin. As I mentioned earlier, when you spread your energy thin, it's all over the place, and progress is *slow*. If you want to dig a well to reach water, for example, it's more efficient to dig one hole 100-feet deep than it is to dig five twenty-foot holes. Narrowing your attention is *leverage*. When you create leverage, manifestation and goal-achievement happens at a quicker rate than you could ever imagine.

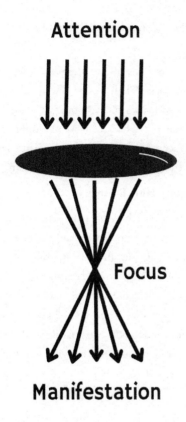

Many of us are chasing false dreams with false expectations. Naturally, this leads to chasing false ideas about how to manifest and create success. We embrace ideas like, "you need to outwork everyone else" or "you need to do *more*." We search far and wide for more tactics, tools, and techniques instead of honing in on the ones we already have. In reality, the key to success is knowing how to achieve *more* by doing *less*. Many of the most successful people in the world don't spend twelve-plus hours a day working (unless it's something they want to do). Rather than running around trying to do everything, they spend their daily supply of energy on the few key tasks.

Focusing on less doesn't give the same dopamine spike that focusing on more does. When we are distracted, something novel, new, or different will always catch our attention. We spend too much time seeking the trivial instead of doubling down on the essentials. We've become *unnecessarily busy*. They say busy is good. But when it's distracting you from living a fulfilling life, is it?

Essential versus Non-Essential

When it comes to achieving your Chief Aim, there are only a few tasks you need to do that will lead to the best results. These small inputs create big outputs. By defining what's essential in your life, you're saying "No" to everything else. This facilitates the manifestation process because you have fewer things to focus on, so you do more of the few. When you segment your attention this way, you maximize your ability to manifest. By narrowing down where you place your attention, you give yourself permission to manifest outcomes with the least amount of effort and the most enjoyment.

If you're going to avoid the infinite distractions that surround you daily, auditing your tasks, opportunities, and decisions is key. Distractions steal your energy, joy, and time without providing a reasonable return. By reducing the amount of decisions you make, you get the biggest bang for your buck. The simplest way to speed up your journey is to make fewer, better decisions with the opportunity and energy you have available to you now. Think of it as an investment.

If your energy is a finite resource, everything you give your energy to is an investment. And just like any investment, you want to maximize your return. You want to make a profit. You want to win big. To do this, you need to know what you're investing in. You need to research the market. When it comes to manifestation, you need to research your life and business. What areas and pillars give you the highest return?

The rest of this chapter is based on the *Pareto Principle*—focusing on the twenty percent of inputs that result in eighty percent of outputs. This is how you make manifestation feel effortless. Most of society focuses on expending trivial, non-essential effort that takes away their energy and joy, leads to insignificant levels of progress, and makes manifestation a struggle. *Just because you can do it all, doesn't mean you should.* By auditing your work and leveraging it, you find the path of least resistance to your goals. Here are three pillars to implement:

1) 80/20 Energy

When you have more energy, you have more freedom. By increasing your energy, you increase the "daily budget" for your investments. Habits and routines such as better-quality sleep, daily exercise, and healthy eating habits can all contribute to increasing your energy. Ask yourself, *What are the few activities that give me the most energy and vitality for the day?*

For example, improving your sleep. Maybe you need to invest in a better mattress and/or blackout curtains. To increase the frequency at which you exercise, if you don't enjoy the gym, perhaps you could go running with a friend or join a sports club. To eat healthier, perhaps you could prepare your meals for the week in advance, so you don't fall for the temptation of eating out. Those are potential examples of how to invest in the twenty percent to realize the eighty percent. An example of "trivial" effort might be tracking your sleep patterns with technology. With exercise, the trivial might be creating rules or boundaries around the type of exercise you need to do. For eating, trivial might be taking certain supplements you can find in whole foods.

By finding the twenty percent that gives you the most energy and investing in it, you're giving yourself the fuel you need to focus on the other two pillars. I see this when I go to the gym or exercise at least twice a week. I've had this simple routine for the past five years, and if it wasn't for this, I would be limiting the amount of energy I could give to my goals.

Another example can be outsourcing tasks that take too much energy away from what's important. By outsourcing work, you free up your attention to focus on other tasks that require deeper levels of concentration and input, thus leading to better outcomes. Energy is the starting point of everything. When you free up your energy, you make bigger investments in the reality you choose to bring to fruition.

2)   80/20 Joy

Joy is the driving force for your creativity, innovation, and flow. The people who find the most flow and focus enjoy the work they do. Remember, humans are purpose-driven beings and we get fulfillment from doing meaningful work. Ironically, our satisfaction doesn't come from traveling, taking vacations, or going out on weekends. Sure, those activities are pleasurable, but they only touch the surface when it comes to authentic, soul-level contentment.

When you find joy in your work, it's easier to focus. If all you did was work on projects that didn't excite you, you didn't care about, and that did nothing meaningful for others, you'd have a difficult time investing your heart into them. *We work to live, we do not live to work.* The goal should never be to stop working or retire. It should be to have the freedom to work on projects that give you joy. That's the ultimate fulfillment.

The United Nations has been publishing the World Happiness Report for over ten years, to measure and track the "where," "what," and "why's" of happiness. The report suggests that unemployed people experience thirty percent more negative emotions in their day-to-day lives. Work goes beyond making money and creating freedom. Work is the backbone of living a fulfilling reality.

So, find work that's in alignment with the reality you want to live. If you spend most of your energy, time, and attention on work, it is to choose work that's in the frequency you want to attract. Think about it. If you can't change jobs, look for elements in your work that you enjoy the most. Focus on those. Change the meaning you give to your work.

Whether we're aware of it or not, the work we do is bettering the life of someone, somewhere. If you're building a house, think about the happy family that will live there. If you're cooking a meal, think about the hungry worker that's going to savor every bite. If you're designing clothes, think about the teenager who will feel more confident in themselves when they wear your designs. By thinking from the end, you'll find your joy.

3) 80/20 Outcomes

There are many people in spiritual communities who have tons of good energy. They love what they do and do what they love. It's admirable and inspiring. However, few of these individuals experience significant physical manifestations resulting from their good energy. They can be the most positive person on the planet and still struggle with paying bills and fulfilling their needs. Why? Because they're not optimizing for results. Although focusing on the process and journey is the most important, outcomes shouldn't be completely discarded.

When the focus falls too much on the first two pillars, we neglect the everyday reality: we need to pay our bills, buy groceries, pay taxes, and support ourselves and others. Remember, while the goal is to free ourselves from the constraints of society, physically, we're still in it. To master your reality is to master even the things you believe are holding humanity back from experiencing more conscious expansion—like struggling to live in our modern, chaotic world. This means mastering the reality of matter. In the world of business, for example, it's understanding value exchange, sales psychology, or product development, or developing a high-income skill. In the world of health, it means eating whole foods, sleeping six to ten hours each night, or taking antibiotics to heal a wound.

By segmenting your energy for optimizing outcomes, and following the other two pillars, you're setting yourself up for an effortless journey to your goals. When you focus on and stick to the essentials, life ceases to be a struggle.

Start with Ugly

"But, Ryuu, how do I know what the twenty percent is?"

A simple way to narrow your attention is to create a long list of tasks, areas, or activities you want to optimize. From there, choose one or two that match your twenty percent criteria, and give your fresh, undivided attention to those. Many times, when we do this exercise, we notice the activities that give us the most energy, joy, and results are the simple, obvious ones. Lay the foundation for your goals as you move toward them. More often than not, doing the mundane, boring, onerous work brings the most progress. Instead of spending time deciding which brick to pick up next, pick any brick and start stacking them.

Thinking is easier than taking action. Each has its importance, and of course, thinking and then doing is where the magic happens. The easiest way to start is to start with the *ugly*. Develop what's known as a "zero-draft" approach—begin creating with minimal structure or focus. Just put words on paper. Any words. Being okay with failing and making mistakes is the easiest way to gain momentum. By narrowing your attention to the ugly, you're focusing on the present moment and your next best steps. The first step isn't always the prettiest. It might be nowhere near what you imagined it to be. And that's okay. It's not supposed to be perfect. It's not supposed to work the first time out. By embracing this mindset, you muffle the voice of your inner critic.

One way to identify when you are shifting is self-acceptance. When you accept where you are, with all your flaws, weaknesses, and inexperience, you give yourself potential to improve. Many people don't improve because they either start projects with an expertise bias or non-acceptance of themselves. Either they think they know it all or they can't be okay with the fact that they don't. Embrace *shoshin* (beginner's mind). It's the only authentic way to grow and improve.

Focused Manifesting

Reality is always in motion—it shifts, bends, and swerves in all kinds of directions. Although there is no such thing as the "perfect moment," timing your decisions and actions is important. Just as the old saying goes, "there's a time and place for everything." Sometimes, you need to wait for certain circumstances before making your next move. This is *patience*. Figure out what to do in the meantime. When starting from scratch, *doing* will always be more productive than waiting and thinking.

Even if you make mistakes, you're taking advantage of the best feedback reality can give you. You learn more from personal experience than you'd learn from any book, course, or teacher. By embracing this mechanism for growth, you can calibrate and find your own approach. The impactful lessons are not the ones we're taught but the ones we learn through application. And as the saying goes, "there's no time like the present" to apply what we have learned.

The only moment that ever exists is now. If you have nothing to work with, *now* is the perfect time to choose something. If you have something to work with, *now* is the perfect time to work on it. The good, the bad, the pretty, and the ugly are all wrapped up in this singular moment of eternal presence—and they are all you have to work with to realize your dreams.

Your journey to goal achievement and manifestation doesn't start in the future or in the past. It's in your everyday, present-moment decisions. The little choices you make today affect tomorrow and beyond. The only person with the power to change your reality is you. You have everything you need to get started, even if it's not up to par with your future standards.

A few months ago, I started my YouTube channel (shameless plug: @MonkModeUniversity). I recorded the first eight videos on my iPhone, in the living rooms of Airbnb's. I didn't wait to get an expensive camera. I didn't wait to find a "video thumbnail guy." I didn't wait until I got settled in my new apartment, until I had a better mic, until I felt confident about speaking, or until I found my editing style. I didn't wait. I just did it, like Nike.

When you know it's the right time to act, the longer you wait, the more doubt you're going to have. Eliminate doubt with action, then iterate as you move along. The path won't always look as glamorous, smooth, or exciting as you cut it out to be. Be okay with this. Accept that the essentials are sometimes the most boring and difficult part of building a dream.

It is through steady forward movement that we see our desires manifest. The path of least resistance isn't complex, intricate, or overwhelming. It's simple. It always will be. When you're disciplined with the twenty percent, results compound. Complexity is difficult to grow and scale. Simplicity isn't.

Manifestation is about meeting the Universe halfway. Sometimes, the path to that halfway point is filled with work that isn't pretty, but it's effective. However, what if it didn't have to be this way? What if the boring was exciting? Imagine how much easier it would be to take action.

Reimagine the Task

The way we look at a task has a profound impact on how we deal with it. If you think a task will be difficult, it will be difficult. If you think it will be boring, it will be boring. Naturally, such perspectives make focusing and completing any task an uphill battle. A distracted mind will never find genuine enjoyment and

Focused Manifesting

flow in work. Your attention will always be on when it's time to "clock out."

Your perspective on what needs to be done to realize a particular outcome influences the actions you take to affect that outcome. When you understand this, you realize that the task itself is not what needs to change, it's your outlook that needs to change. Reimagine the task itself. No task has a singular meaning. It can be enjoyable or boring, depending on how the person doing the task engages with it. Does this mean we have to learn to "love the process?" Not necessarily. Of course, it you love the process, you'd perform the task well with ease. Still, enjoying something that doesn't come easily, or that you've never been interested in, can be difficult. Here's how we can make this a reality.

First, we can develop *curiosity* about the task. Are there details involved you have not considered? Can you optimize the doing of the task so you're more efficient or effective? What can you add to or remove from the task to make it more enjoyable? Approach any task as you would a game. When you question the minutiae involved in doing a task, you focus on it more. *Curiosity breeds focus*. And when you're focused, you're in flow.

For example, how can you make lawn mowing more enjoyable? You can learn everything there is to know about lawn mowing. Research the different models of lawn mowers and the different grasses. Test to find the most optimal path to cut the lawn. Track your time with every test. Are there specific rituals or secondary tasks you can do before or after you mow to improve the process? The more intensely you focus on a task, the more interesting it becomes, and vice versa.

The next layer to reimagining the task is introducing *novelty*. When a task feels mundane or repetitive, you might resist doing it. Your mind seeks the dopamine hit that comes from other, more exciting things. To surrender yourself to doing something repetitive isn't easy. You get into the habit of starting then stopping, and you force yourself to complete the task. One way of introducing novelty into your work is by changing the location at which you work. This is why co-working spaces have become a revolutionary way of working. Every time you go to work, you see different people, and sit in a different seat. Maybe you even work at different times of day. When you're starving for inspiration, change your location. Even if it's just inside your home or office, move things around in your workspace. Sit at a different side of the table or rearrange the furniture so every work day *looks* and *feels* like a new day.

The last layer in reimagining a task is to *connect the dots* between things you enjoy and the work you find difficult to do. This is like the first layer, whereby you approach the task like it's a game, only now, you correlate the task itself with an interest you have. For example, during the process of producing my earlier books, I sometimes lacked inspiration about how I wanted to approach each book and what I wanted to include in it. In one book, there was no structure to the outline, it was just a bunch of information. Naturally, this caused me to get distracted by other things—one being watching football. As a kid, I loved building imaginary teams, whether through a video game or in a real-life game with friends. I'd pretend to be one of my favorite players, and this made the sport more exciting. I'd let my imagination run rampant, which often led to me playing a better game. I got into *flow*.

As I reflected on this, I thought about how I could fuse the world of football with the world of books. Since there's no physicality involved, I knew I'd need to approach it with my head, sort of like a manager. That was my lightbulb moment. I realized that each of my books is like a team in my league. Every chapter is a player on the roster. My purpose with the books was to win the game (or in book terms, to affect a reader and earn a fan). I had to make sure my defense was good, and that at the end of the book, readers had no questions. I also wanted to score goals and give readers insights they'd never heard before. When I connected the dots between these two worlds, everything made sense. I knew what I needed to do, and doing it was enjoyable.

By reimagining a task, you create a whole new world for your work. Narrow your attention to a parallel reality in which the hard tasks are easy and where your imagination takes charge and serves as a guidepost for innovation, creativity, and action.

In the next chapter, we're going to look at how you can use this redefined state of purpose and action to create your own luck.

CHAPTER 9 EXERCISES

80/20 Energy

In your life, what 20% of habits give you 80% of your energy?

80/20 Joy

In your life, what 20% of activities give you 80% of your joy?

Focused Manifesting

80/20 Outcomes

In your work, what 20% of tasks give you 80% of your outcomes?

Defining Your Ugly Tasks

Write down a list of tasks you don't feel like doing, are tired of doing, or have no interest in doing.

Reimagining the Ugly

Next to each task above,

a) write down small details you haven't accounted for or studied.

b) write down ways you can introduce novelty to them.

Focused Manifesting

c) write down how you can relate them to subjects you enjoy.

CHAPTER 10

REALIGNING YOUR FOCUS

Law #10:
You Create Your Own Luck

"You have to create your own luck. You have to be aware of the opportunities around you and take advantage of them."

Bruce Lee

Focused Manifesting

Do you sometimes feel you're cursed or that the world is against you? No matter how hard you try, does it always feel like there's something standing in the way of your dreams? For most people, there's plenty of evidence to support this notion. But if you flip the perspective, you can propel yourself to new heights you never thought possible. *The Universe will always meet your expectations.* If you expect the world to rain on your parade, there will be clouds on the horizon. But when you shift your awareness from *what is going wrong* to *what is going right*, you notice your "good luck" and attract more of it.

The lesson of this chapter is *irrational optimism*. This isn't the same as "optimistic denial," which is when you pretend everything is okay when in reality it's falling apart. People also refer to this as "toxic positivity," but I don't like that phrase because it's an oxymoron. Positivity can't ever be toxic because if it were, it would no longer be positive.

Optimistic denial is when you ignore facts because you hold a (false) belief that by pretending to be happy and rejecting reality, you can dodge your way to success. This isn't how it works. Pivoting your perspective differs from blinding yourself to reality. When we blind ourselves, we're in hiding. When we're hiding, we're resisting what's present. And, as the old saying goes, *what you resist...*

A better approach is to train yourself on where you choose to place your attention. The human brain has a powerful pattern-recognizing mechanism, and those patterns create our existence. We know this mechanism as the Reticular Activating System (RAS). The RAS connects the subconscious mind with the conscious mind. It brings to light that which we're seeking. The more we focus on something, the more often we're going to see it. An example of this is when you decide on the next car you'd like to purchase, and shortly after, start seeing it everywhere. The goal of the RAS is to seek information, evidence, and proof to validate your current beliefs and intentions. This happens automatically, without you having to do anything. When properly set up, this mechanism can revolutionize how you engage with reality.

Since ancient times, we human beings have trained ourselves to see the negative in everything. This is called the "negativity bias." Our goal as a species has always been to survive, not thrive. From an evolutionary perspective, being positively inclined is a fast way to death. In nature, if you're not watching your back or studying the scene with care, you might end up in the digestive track of a predator. Therefore, our minds are trained to focus on the "dangers" of life. However, life nowadays is safe compared to what our ancestors had to go through. This means that the negativity bias does us more harm than good. Of course, if you're alone in the middle of a sketchy neighborhood at 3:00 a.m., be vigilant. That said, don't carry this vigilance into your home, work, or relationships.

Animals of all kinds live in the present moment. They are simply being, non-judgmentally. What differentiates humans from all other animals is our ability to think about and reflect on the past and future. We add all our deadlines, events, workloads, meetings, tasks, and errands to our symphony of priorities, overloading our nervous systems with objects of focus that steal our attention. This overload of information weakens our ability to be conscious. When we have many distractions, we lose our capacity to control and manage where we place our attention. Feeling out of control will often put us in a state of stress, or *survival mode*. Once we're in this state, our animal mind takes over, putting our RAS to work—against our intentions. Before we know it, it feels like everything is working against us. We think we're "out of luck." We give attention to narratives that not

Focused Manifesting

only distract us, but reenforce the negative patterns of the RAS, thus attracting the very reality we're trying to avoid.

The trick is to retrain your mind from "what's going wrong" to "what's going right," from "why is this not working?" to "how can we make this work?" and from "I don't want this" to "I intend to have that." This isn't about ignoring the challenges in your life (these you still have to face head-on) it's about shifting your attention to the reality you want to attract. It's about pivoting your attention toward the ideas, thoughts, and perspectives that propel you toward your desired reality, reinterpreting the "facts" to play in your favor.

Maybe you didn't close as many clients as you thought you would. Maybe you didn't sell as many copies of your book as you thought you would. Pay close attention to these "unmet" expectations, because they might put you on a path to a more sustainable and surprising manifestation. Always remember, the Universe will never grant you anything for which you aren't a vibrational match. Use the feedback the Universe giving you to *realign your focus*.

The road to manifesting is never a straight line. The Universe has many surprises in store for you. You may not see, hear, smell, taste, or touch them, but they are there. Once you reinterpret the meaning behind your challenges, obstacles, and setbacks, you'll notice internal changes. These changes will give you the opportunity to develop your thinking, shed your limitations, and grow as an individual. With this internal change, a change in luck will also come.

The same way you can come up with 100 reasons something "can't" or "won't" work, is the same way you need to come up with 100 reasons it "can" and "will." Where is the positive in the supposed negative? I call this the *Appreciation Abundance* exercise. Again, it's not about rejecting reality, it's about using reality as feedback for changing your thoughts and actions. By making these small shifts, you're training yourself to rest your attention on the reality you want to grow. The fact you're getting any feedback at all is an event to celebrate. Most people don't get feedback from their reality because they don't input anything. If you input nothing, how can you expect output? And even if you give your energy to something, if you're not focused and you're distracted by shiny objects, you may not notice the signs the Universe is trying to give you.

There was a time in my life when nothing was going right. Looking back now, I see it was because I had a ton of *distractions*. It was easy to keep my mind in the negative loop that kept confirming itself in my external reality. I spent many days drinking, smoking, and hanging around people and environments that did nothing for me but make me feel less confident and more anxious. The moment I cleared myself of all those distractions was the moment I had enough mental space to reconsider my interpretation of reality. I was no longer giving energy to the pendulums that kept me stuck. My thoughts, perspectives, and beliefs came into question, because now, it was just me, myself, and I. I was no longer the victim of an external perspective, but a *chooser* of my own.

Remember the twin brothers who each chose a different life because their father was an alcoholic? Like them, you're already living your own personal myth. Your parents, teachers, and authority figures told you the myth, and your peers reinforced it. However, the myth is only as true as you believe it to be, and as with the twins, you too have the power to redefine your myth. When you become the chooser of your perspective, you become the creator of your reality. Sometimes you have to see yourself like David and your reality like Goliath. On paper, you stand no chance. But that's just on paper. Out on the field, it's a whole different game.

If you prepare yourself beforehand, any possibility can be a reality. Notice how I didn't say "if you believe, any possibility can be a reality." Because how can you believe if you don't prepare? How can you believe if you don't follow any of the steps or actions I've shared in this book? Belief is difficult to build without evidence.

Noticing the Space

Subconsciously, the mind is always looking for evidence to prove that its perspective of reality is the right one. This is the work of the RAS. When you give attention to an object of focus, you perpetuate its presence. The mind seeks proof of the beliefs it carries. This is the ego part of your mind. The ego will always want to be proven right, to stay secure, and to remain in the "know." If you want to shift your perspective, first you need to let go of your old worldview. To do this, you need to be okay with "not knowing." This means being open to more possibilities than the ones your ego can conjure up. When an event happens, your mind will give it a *meaning* to create evidence to defend its beliefs. Ideally, you want this meaning to be positive. But that doesn't happen all the time. With every experience, we always have the choice to place a new meaning onto it. We shouldn't always allow our mind to make this call for us. In the legendary book, *Man's Search for Meaning*, Victor Frankl speaks on the idea of a space that exists between stimulus and response.

"Between stimulus and response, there is a space. In that space lies our freedom and our power to choose our response. In our response lies our growth and our happiness."

Victor Frankl

One key to letting go of an old thought, perspective, or habit is to give yourself the space to experience the space. In this emptiness, you have not decided yet on the meaning you'll place on the event or stimulus. Be comfortable in this space. Again, let not knowing feel comfortable.

Our minds are in a great rush to find evidence to prove themselves right. The more we can slow down the mind, the easier it will be to shift the evidence that confirms a new reality. And by giving the mind fresh evidence, you confirm to it that it can adopt a different perception of reality, which will change the evidence it seeks next time around. *Seek the evidence first and the mind will follow your lead.*

It all starts with conscious intention. In the beginning, do not notice the space between stimulus and response in moments of chaos. This is far too difficult if you haven't trained yourself first. Before a pilot can set foot on a plane, he or she must go through flight simulation training. The same concept can apply here. Before you're faced with a circumstance that would make you reactive and negative, journal about the main events happening in your life right now. What's the worst-case scenario? What's the best-case scenario? List all the positive evidence you can generate from both potential realities.

Having the right perspective when everything is going your way is easy. The hard part is when you're faced with circumstances that make you believe everything is going to crash down. When you prepare yourself for the worst, it's easier to focus on your desired reality.

Another form of noticing the space between stimulus and response is by giving more attention to the practice of *gratitude*. Gratitude is the "mother of all virtues," and when you incorporate it into your life, you can change your world for the better. Most

Focused Manifesting

people who practice gratitude do so mentally. They "think" about their blessings. They "think" about how well things in their lives are going, and while this isn't a bad thing, it isn't experiencing gratitude for what it is: *a feeling*.

Once you have identified something in your life that makes you feel grateful, ask yourself "Why does this make me grateful? What other emotions does it make me feel?" You'll notice many nuanced emotions arising that you didn't realize were comforting and reassuring, and that put you into the right state of consciousness and focus. The more you tune into this frequency, the more you vibrate in tandem with that which you wish to manifest.

When you use gratitude as a filter for your life, you'll notice that you're surrounded by blessings. Obstacles disappear, successes happen, and before you know it, reality molds into your dream. While it's fine to start small, understand this: you can never be grateful enough. There is always something for which to be grateful, and by stacking your blessings and keeping them close to your heart, you maintain awareness, always looking for evidence that more of the same—more blessings and more good luck—is coming your way.

Now let's look into how we can use these newly found blessings to bring your Chief Aim to fruition.

Connecting the Dots

In the film industry, the term "canon" describes the most authentic, relevant part of any storyline. For example, that Darth Vader reveals his identity to Luke Skywalker in the movie *Star Wars* is not only important, it is essential to the storyline. If this moment didn't happen, the sequence of events would have turned out differently for Luke. Darth Vader's revelation is canon to the Star Wars story.

The same way movies have canon events that define the outcome of the movie, you want to create canon events that define the destiny of your *life*. What do I mean by this? Well, think about something good that happened to you recently. Other than it being a blessing, think about how you can define the event in a way that links with your Chief Aim. The way most people notice blessings is through a lens of gratitude. However, if you want to take it one step further, show *appreciation* for the blessing. Don't just sit with it, use the blessing to your advantage. Connect it with your Chief Aim. Reinterpret the blessing so it fuels the path you've chosen. Here's an example: *A publishing house reached out to publish my new book.*

Most people would respond to that declaration with the thought: "That is great news!" and leave it at that. A more powerful way to interpret a blessing like this would be: "This is great! I must be a superb writer and communicator." Notice how you're using the blessing as *confirmation* of your manifestation. You're confirming that you're on the right path and that you are who you say you are. By connecting the dots, you're reaffirming that you are making progress toward your goal and the identity you want to embody.

This is why daily gratitude journaling can be such a powerful tool. It trains your mind to see the connection between a "good event" and the goal you want to achieve. Most people will write down what they're grateful for. But an even more powerful way of realigning your focus is by linking what you're grateful for with what you want to achieve. Don't hold back with this.

* I wrote fifty words for my book today. I'm becoming a best-selling author.*

* I spoke on stage today. I'm becoming a full-time public speaker.*

Focused Manifesting

*   I found ten dollars in my pocket today. I'm attracting an avalanche of abundance.*

Exaggerate your win. Relish in it. By doing this, you're giving more attention and energy to that which you want to attract. The more evidence you have that proves you are on the right path, the less energy you'll spend worrying, doubting, chasing, or feeling a sense of lack.

Another way to approach this is using canon events from your personal history and linking them with your Chief Aim. Again, you are rewriting your personal narrative. You can see this technique play out when people connect their romantic relationships with their success in business. Had they not met that special someone, they wouldn't be where they are in their career. This is just one dimension of this practice of connecting dots. *Use your success in one area of life to confirm your potential for reaching success in all the others.*

It may take some time for you to reflect on this. You'll need to go back and write out an entire catalog of your accomplishments, wins, and successes, and transform them into confirmations. But it'll be worth it. When you realize how much evidence you have, you'll never go back to doubting your potential. If believing is productive, doubting is a distraction.

Don't stop here. Can you can apply this technique to your past failures? What lessons did you learn? What fresh path did your failure put you on? Because you are reading this right now, you are an ambitious person. Ambition isn't born out of nowhere. It comes from an underlying lack of fulfillment in your current circumstances. It's wanting to be, live, and experience more than you have been, in every sense of the word. Ambition comes from experiencing the opposite, from experiencing the days of no purpose, lack of passion, inconsistent action, and distracted thoughts. Experiencing the lows gives you the fuel to experience the highs.

> *"If you had to create a human, what would you put them through to make them tough? It probably wouldn't be a chill life. What would you put them through to make them patient? You probably wouldn't give them things immediately. We want these traits, but each of them has a price tag attached to it."*

Alex Hormozi

If you've paid the price necessary to develop a character trait and are still paying it, give yourself permission to embody and develop the trait. Use your suffering as a tool for growth. Connect the dots of suffering and growth, and nothing you go through will be meaningless. It will always correlate with your ultimate goal.

Developing Willpower

Realigning your focus requires conscious effort. It requires taking hold of the thing that allows you to focus your mind in the direction you want it to go: willpower. Without exercising your willpower, you could not succeed at anything I have outlined so far in this book. This is the foremost ability required to change the habits of mind that direct ninety percent of the actions you take daily. By developing willpower, you're better able to harness your attention. It's a necessary skill to develop in order to move past that first layer of resistance you experience whenever you're caught in a loop of distractions and negative thinking. Think of willpower as a muscle and your attention like a boulder. When you're moving a boulder (attention), you're picking it up with your

Focused Manifesting

muscles (willpower) and placing it in the location you choose. The better developed your willpower is, the lighter the boulder will feel, the quicker you'll it pick up, and the faster you'll get to the new location. Willpower is the muscle of your mind, and just like any muscle, it needs to be trained through repetition and consistency. Here are three ways you can develop your willpower:

1)   Finish what you start.

One of the best ways of developing willpower is to finish what you start. Most people give up halfway. They dabble. This is why most people aren't where they want to be. Knowing "how to quit" is a topic I've talked about in other books, but for our purposes here, finishing what you start is a great way to develop the willpower you need to thrive in this Universe of distractions.

There will be times when it doesn't matter how much you optimize your environment, routine, or habits, you'll need willpower to realign with your chosen focus. Developing a "begin and finish" mentality is great for training this muscle.

2)   Do more than you think you can.

This comes down to raising your standards. When you have little willpower, it's easy to sell yourself short and underestimate the amount of energy you have. A few months ago, I struggled with only being able to write for one to two hours each day. The coffee crashes and lack of inspiration were coming faster than usual. I was making consistent progress, but I knew I could do more, especially if I wanted to finish this project faster. So, whenever I felt like I had done "enough," I extended my work time by thirty minutes. It wasn't an enormous difference, but it was enough to convince myself that I did indeed have enough energy to continue.

The subconscious mind is a powerful tool to automate and facilitate transformation. Developing habits and routines that align with your goals is the simplest way of setting yourself up to succeed. However, be aware of this mechanism. The same way it can help put you on the right path, it can also keep you stuck on the wrong one. Do not let your subconscious mind hold you back from stretching your capabilities.

3) Do better than you think you can.

When we are producing work of any sort, we have a certain level of expectation of our abilities. For example, we accept the fact that we are at a "beginner" or "intermediate" level. When we label ourselves in this way, sometimes it holds us back from reaching the next level. To reach the next level in any area, we need to develop the next level of focus. This means using our willpower to put in a little more work than we do usually. Studying a subject just a tad bit deeper. Slowing down our reps a bit. Tweaking the design to give it that extra edge. When we do better, we become better.

Realigning your focus is all about understanding that your perspectives create your luck. When you train yourself through willpower to optimize your worldview, you're giving energy to the reality you want to experience.

In the next chapter, we'll be placing the cherry on top and helping you hone in on the one thing that makes you stand out from the rest.

CHAPTER 10 EXERCISES

Noticing the Space

What moments throughout your day do you negatively react to? Write down what you'd like your new response to be for each. Remember to apply Viktor Frankl's technique.

_____

_____

_____

_____

_____

Creating Evidence

What's working for you in life right now? Write down a list of areas you're doing well in and succeeding at.

_____

_____

_____

_____

_____

Connecting Dots

Next to each piece of evidence listed above, explain how it's getting you closer to your Chief Aim. Connect the dots.

Developing Willpower

a) What are some projects or tasks that you've initiated but not yet completed?

b) In which areas do you believe you have the potential to increase your contributions or efforts?

c) In what aspects of your work or personal life do you think you have the capacity to improve the quality of your output?

CHAPTER 11

HONING IN

Law #11: Success Loves Masters

"In order to master a field, you must love the subject and feel a profound connection to it. Your interest must transcend the field itself and border on the religious."

Robert Greene

Throughout this book, we've covered fundamental principles on how to remain laser focused to manifest anything you set your mind to. However, there is one ultimate principle that will wrap up everything we've talked about so far. In the first chapter, we spoke about your Chief Aim and focusing on your inner levers—like your strengths, obsessions, excitement, and belief system. However, applying these concepts is easier said than done.

In a world that offers everyone more options and possibilities than ever before, finding your "one thing" can be difficult and intimidating. We know that in order to be successful, we need to commit to a career, business, or idea for the long-term. Dabbling, as we've discussed, gets you nowhere. If there's one thing that the most successful people in the world have in common, it's that they've mastered *at least* one thing.

Mastery is not a trait you're born with. You develop and refine it over a time. All industries respect mastery. The main reason is because it's *rare*. For example, you can see people's appreciation of mastery when they admire elaborate, well-known art pieces. Even if you know nothing about art, it's easy to be impressed with a master's work. Back in the day, blacksmiths illustrated the concept of master craftmanship well. They required extensive training and years (sometimes decades) of apprenticeship. Once they were skilled enough, they became journeymen, and traveled far and wide to train under other masters, taking years to prove themselves. Once they were skilled enough in the eyes of their masters, they earned the title "master blacksmith." In any modern-day profession, masters develop in a similar fashion.

Mastery is a direct route to effortless manifestation. Imagine how much easier it is to make money as a skilled salesperson, to get court wins as an expert lawyer, or to have diners coming back to enjoy more of your food when you are a proficient chef. When you're a master, you become magnetic to opportunities. Success loves masters. Now it's just a matter of choosing what to be a master in.

Double Down on Your Calling

When it comes to talents, they are finite. While you might have an infinite number of options to choose from, the truth is most people have three to five main natural talents with which, with less effort, they do better than the average person. *What areas, traits, and skills come to you easily? What do you have a natural inclination for?* This is the first layer of mastery—your calling. While you have the power to do whatever you want, in reality, you can't do everything you want. For example, a middle-aged, 5'9" man can decide he wants to pursue a career as a player in the NBA (National Basketball Association), but the likelihood of that happening are slim to none, no matter how much he applies the principle of manifestation. There are two elements you need to consider when choosing your path of mastery— *talent* and *timing*.

The biggest frustration someone can experience is trying to be something they are not. When you go against the grain of your biological and spiritual DNA, you're choosing the path of most resistance and ego. Avoid choosing a path for the wrong reasons (e.g., money, fame, status, validation). While it might be "cool" to be a famous DJ, for example, maybe your natural talent is with numbers and mathematics. Does this mean you should ditch the idea of ever being involved with DJ-ing? Of course not. The key is to find harmony between your talents and interests. Become the financial director of a big music label. Become the personal accountant of a famous DJ. Work with music venues to manage their cash flow. Fuse your talents with your interests. You'll soon find out that working on your calling is where real joy comes from.

The path to mastery is the path of greatest fulfillment. When you master something, you learn to love it. It feels good to be exceptional. It feels good to do work that calls you and comes naturally. When people see the work you do, they're in awe, even if the work is not something you ever saw yourself doing. It's funny. It's often assumed that we get to choose our purpose. But the reality is, *it chooses us.*

When I was a kid, I never thought for one second of becoming an author. I loved football, was decent at math, and have a knack for writing. My inclination was toward games that required tactics, strategies, and teams. I was clueless about the publishing industry. My friends and family members were surprised when they found out I write books and coach for a living. Why did I decide to stick to it? Well, the simple answer is, I was good at it, people liked it, and it gave me the life I wanted to live. Would I say that writing is my only life's passion? No. Do I derive immense satisfaction from my work? One hundred percent. I enjoy writing AND it gives me the life I want. It's my path of mastery. The path that will help me create, build, and manifest the life I want. I didn't choose this path, it chose me. So, I embrace it, go all-in, and use it to fulfill all of my other interests and passions.

There are two ways of finding your calling. The first is by looking back at your childhood. *Where did your inclinations and curiosity lie? What games and subjects called to you the most? What were you most curious about?* The second is by looking at the path you're on now. *Where do you excel effortlessly? What type of work feels good and comes to you easily?* By doing this self-analysis, you can understand where you should put your focus.

It's never too late to pursue your path of mastery. It doesn't matter how deep you are in your career or business, you can always redirect. You are not wedded to your past choices. By letting go of your initial plan, you open up space for a new, exciting adventure.

Mastery doesn't go away. It's with you until the day you die. When you embody the traits of a master, those traits will be there to help you whenever you need them. This is why people who are good in business aren't afraid of risk. They know if they lose it all, they can build it up again. This is also why they succeed more often than not. When it comes to a job, even if you were to lose it, you would still have the skills and repertoire to apply for and find another one. Mastery, once developed, never dies. It's the best way to be consistent with manifestation.

As you travel your path of mastery, you will be tempted to deviate. Other paths and distractions will show themselves (and may even make you wild promises). To your ego, they will sound like great deals, but in fact they will only steer you off your path. The greatest distractions to mastery are boredom, impatience, fear, and confusion. Once you overcome these hurdles, you'll be well on your way.

Boredom

In Chapter 9, we spoke about the idea of starting with the ugly and how to overcome the resistance that comes with it. On top of this, you need to accept that the path to mastery will require extensive repetition. Once you accept this and apply the principles we've addressed, you'll be well on your way to becoming a master.

Impatience

Mastery takes time. When it comes to excelling in any field, you always want to approach it with the long term in mind. A person playing a ten-year game will always accomplish more than someone who quits after the first year. This is why knowing how to choose your field is so important. It will be what you do for much of your life.

Fear

A master's journey begins with excitement and curiosity, but it can also bring fear about how much there is to learn. It can intimidate you in the early stages. So it's important that you accustom yourself to having a beginner's mind. When you can be okay with not knowing everything and value learning over everything else, you can overcome this initial resistance.

Confusion

We live in a world of information abundance. Everyone has access to information. Therefore, the difference between a master and everyone else is that a master has what's known as *specific knowledge*. This is knowledge that's gained through pursuing your calling. It's technical, it's creative, and no one can teach it to you. It's knowledge you can only learn by creating, failing, and iterating. Instead of thinking about what you should do, just start. From there, everything will become clearer.

Once you discover your calling, you need to home in on the specific skills and traits that will make this calling a part of your everyday reality. This isn't about developing another hobby or side project. It's about prioritizing your life's work, and turning it into something that can support you spiritually and financially.

Blending Interest with Impact

In order to become a master, you must have a game plan. World-class athletes don't become the best without having a blueprint for their success. They understand their end goal and they understand what they need to do to excel in their field. A professional surfer will do different exercises than a football player. To become the best, it's essential to know what muscle groups to work on and the type of training required. When you're specific about the skills you need to learn, mastery is easier to accomplish.

Athletes know which specific physical traits require more attention than others. For example, a short-distance sprinter and a long-distance runner train differently. A short-distance sprinter wants to increase their leg strength and explosiveness to maximize their output in a short time. As a result, they are far more muscular than long-distance runners, who are leaner because they're more focused on endurance and their running form.

When you find your calling, notice what the essential skills you need to develop are in order to stand out from the rest. For your craft, there's the knowledge of the craft itself and then there's the knowledge of how to distribute, sell, or deliver that craft. You can be a master at what you do, but if nobody knows who you are and why it's important, you won't make the impact you hope for or expect.

In my life, wanting to build a business and studying the Law of Attraction philosophy inspired me to write books that resonated and connected with readers. After receiving tens of thousands of positive comments, I'm convinced that the content is good. However, there was still another skill I needed to develop if I was ever going to stand out from the crowd. This was the art of copywriting. On top of knowing the subject, I needed to learn how to package it. Naturally, this gave me the edge in a market that was "saturated." Had I dabbled and stuck to one muscle group or skill (in this case, mastering the philosophy), I would have blended in with all the other creators in my marketplace.

> *"I fear not the man who has practiced 10,000 kicks once, but I fear the man who has practiced one kick 10,000 times."*

Bruce Lee

If you want to become a master at business, start by mastering one component at a time. It's not vast, general knowledge that will make you stand out—specific knowledge in one domain will. By becoming above average at one thing, you give yourself leverage to move and give attention to the next skill.

When it comes to manifestation, you don't attract what you want, you attract who you are. Therefore, the focus must be to become the version of you that attracts the life you want. Now, this version of you doesn't need to master fifty unique skills to create a shift in your frequency. Becoming a master at *one thing* is enough to make a shift in your reality. Continue on this path, with two to three more skills, and before you know it, your life will be radically different.

This perspective falls in tandem with the *Ikigai* philosophy: Do what you love, what you're good at, what the world needs, and what others can pay you for. This way, you develop mastery in a skill you can use to propel your career forward. Find your obsession. Then learn sales, marketing, and copywriting to sell it—or else you'll be another broke, talented artist.

Do More Than Expected

Many people cringe at the idea of "doing more" and "going the distance." After all, the promise that the Law of Attraction sells us is that we can achieve our desires *effortlessly*—and what I explained above sounds like a ton of effort, right? However, understand

Focused Manifesting

that this is only the mind trying to overcomplicate things. The entire purpose of this book is to help you find your focus, reduce distractions, and hone in for better results. Although we've spoken about subjects that go beyond mere manifestation, these concepts allow us to optimize our approach further. Once you understand the basics of the Law of Attraction, the tweaks and adjustments help you stay consistent and focused.

There is value in being obsessive, just like there is value in having no attachments. It's a matter of balancing both to speed up your path. Understand, deep down, you are already complete, but you can use your natural inclinations to build a world of more abundance, joy, and freedom for yourself and others. It's the idea of needing nothing to be happy and playing the game of life because you want to play.

One way to stand out in this game is by *doing more than what's expected of you*. In a world filled with followers, you can stand out by becoming a *leader*. You do this by taking your endeavors and projects to a whole new creative realm. Many of us like to play it safe and do the same old, same old. It's no wonder that for most people, things don't take off. They're not stretching their boundaries.

When you develop mastery of a subject, it's common to experience a sort of creative atrophy. The moment you think you "know" is the moment you lose curiosity and stop expanding. This is one reason science textbooks are slow to update. It requires an extensive amount shedding and deconstruction of old beliefs and systems in order to introduce new ones.

When you remain curious, you continue to discover new ways of viewing the subject you're experienced in—going down new rabbit holes and having new creative insights. There are new ways to interpret old data, and old processes that can innovate new technologies. It's just a matter of being open and allowing yourself to sink into the subject. In reality, there is nothing truly original. Everything anyone can think of exists within the collective imagination. Anything we can observe, even mentally, already exists. Therefore, any invention, service, software, etc. exists prior to it manifesting into this world. This means that whatever we think about derives from or is inspired by another thought that's manifested.

When we extend our field of study, we open ourselves up to finding timeless principles that span multiple disciplines. I call this *focused exploration.* It's about exploring other niches intending to download insights that apply to your niche. For example, many of the ideas I generated for this book came from studying productivity and time management books and concepts. As I was going through this material, I noticed the connection between these topics and the Law of Attraction. My conclusion was that *developing your focus is a spiritual practice.* The most spiritually evolved humans on this planet understand this to be true. They can maintain concentration and place their awareness on the reality they choose to grow and expand. When you become conscious of your awareness, you can master your mind, and through this, master your reality.

Being a perpetual learner is fundamental for creation, and therefore there is a lot of merit in understanding your industry, niche, or passion. By doing this, you can create solutions to problems that haven't been solved yet, making your creations a valuable offering in your marketplace.

In the final stage of mastery, your goal is to disrupt your industry, to where you inspire change, growth, expansion, and progress. There are infinite ways of approaching a specific topic. Many of them don't resonate because most people are trying to create something they *think* people want. However, the approaches that resonate the most are those that come from Source. They come when you find your *authentic voice*.

In your creative journey in business or in your career, you need to understand that *you* are the niche. Being you is what makes you valuable. Take advantage of this to create and hone in on your own unique trajectory within an industry. Be you (everyone else is taken).

The biggest obstacles to mastery and authenticity are the distractions that steer you away from who you are. Goals, people, and ideas that aren't aligned with your calling are manipulating your focus. When you can outline your unique internal blueprint and use it to guide you on your journey, you'll find that things work out in your favor. It might be scary. It might be uncomfortable. But, when you follow your purpose and creative impulses with full faith, things work out in ways you could never have imagined. Focus solves many of life's most challenging problems. When you define what's important, reduce what isn't, and hone in on your gifts, manifestation becomes inevitable.

CHAPTER 11 EXERCISES

Natural Strengths

What are your natural strengths? (Note: Take the Myer's Briggs Personality Test to find out)

Childhood Interests

What have you always been naturally curious about since you were a child?

Focused Manifesting

Areas of Mastery

What are the specific fields or aspects of your personal and professional life where you feel a deep passion and commitment, with the intention of devoting your lifetime to attain mastery in them?

Skills of A Master

What are the essential skills you need to develop to become a master at your craft or area of interest?

A Short Message From The Author

Hey there, did you enjoy the book? Hopefully you did!

A lot of work, research, and collaborations took place to make this book what it is today. So, if you enjoyed *Focused Manifesting*, I'd love to hear your thoughts in the review section on Amazon.com. It helps me gain valuable feedback to produce the highest quality content for all of my beautiful readers. Even just a short 1-2 sentence review would mean the WORLD to me.

\>> Scan the QR Code above to leave short review on Amazon <<

Thank you from the bottom of my heart for purchasing and reading it to end.

Sincerely,

Ryuu

BIBLIOGRAPHY

16 Personalities. "Free Personality Test." Accessed December 12, 2023. https://www.16personalities.com/free-personality-test

Arens, Elisabeth A., Peter Zeier, Christiane Schwieren, Hanna Huisgen, and Sven Barnow. "The Perils of Aiming Too High: Discrepancy between Goals and Performance in Individuals with Depressive Symptoms." *Journal of Behavior Therapy and Experimental Psychiatry* no. 58 (2018): 12-17. https://doi.org/10.1016/j.jbtep.2017.07.002

BrainyQuote. "Bruce Lee Quote." Accessed December 12, 2023. https://www.brainyquote.com/quotes/bruce_lee_413509

Branson, Richard. *Losing My Virginity: How I Survived, Had Fun, and Made a Fortune Doing Business My Way.* New York: Crown Publishing, 2011.

Clear, James. "Continuous Improvement: How It Works and How to Master It." Accessed December 12, 2023. https://jamesclear.com/continuous-improvement

De Neve, Jan-Emmanuel, and George Ward "Does Work Make You Happy? Evidence from the World Happiness Report". Accessed December 12, 2023. https://hbr.org/2017/03/does-work-make-you-happy-evidence-from-the-world-happiness-report

Frankl, Viktor E. *Man's Search for Meaning.* New York: Simon and Schuster, 1985.

Goddard, Neville. *The Law of Assumption.* Andura Publishing, 2020. Kindle.

Greene, Robert. *Master.* London: Penguin Books, 2013.

Hormozi, Alex. "The Man that Makes Millionaires: How to Turn $1,000 into $100 Million!" *All The Diary Of A CEO Episodes*, April 3, 2023. https://www.youtube.com/watch?v=x3e73Qn6NOo

Keller, Gary, and Jay Papasan. *The ONE Thing: The Surprisingly Simple Truth About Extraordinary Results.* Rooksley Milton Keynes: Bard Press, 2013.

Kershner, Irvin, dir. "Star Wars: The Empire Strikes Back". Gary Kurtz, prod. Twentieth Century Fox, 1980.

Marcelo Dalbosco (@marcelodalbosco.tattoo), "Lisbon Microrealism Tattoo," Instagram, December 12, 2023, https://www.instagram.com/marcelodalbosco.tattoo/

Maxwell, John C. *Intentional Living: Choosing a Life That Matters.* New York: Center Street, 2015. Kindle.

Proctor, Bob. *You Were Born Rich: Now You Can Discover and Develop Those Riches.* Scottsdale: LifeSuccess Productions, 1997.

Quotefancy. "Bruce Lee Quote." Accessed December 12, 2023. https://quotefancy.com/quote/778700/Bruce-Lee-You-have-to-create-your-own-luck-You-have-to-be-aware-of-the-opportunities

Ravikant, Naval. "Desire Is a Contract You Make to Be Unhappy." The Joe Rogan Experience, February 10, 2020. Podcast. Accessed [e.g., YouTube]. [Timestamp: 1:09].

Scroggs, Laura. "The Pomodoro Technique." Accessed December 12, 2023. https://todoist.com/productivity-methods/pomodoro-technique

Shinohara, Ryuu. *The Magic of Manifesting: 15 Advanced Techniques To Attract Your Best Life, Even If You Think It's Impossible Now (Law of Attraction Book 1),* 2019. Kindle.

Watts, Tyler W., Greg J. Duncan, and Haonan Quan. "Revisiting the Marshmallow Test: A Conceptual Replication Investigating Links between Early Delay of Gratification and Later Outcomes." *Psychological Science* 29, no. 7 (2018): 1159-1177. https://doi.org/10.1177/09567976187616

Weidner, Gerdi. "Why Do Men Get More Heart Disease than Women? An International Perspective." *Journal of American College Health* 48, no. 6 (2000): 291-294. https://doi.org/110.1080/07448480009596270

WikiHow. "How to Burn Paper Safely." Accessed December 12, 2023. https://www.wikihow.com/Burn-Paper-Safely

Wordnik. "Harmony." Accessed December 12, 2023. https://www.wordnik.com/words/harmony

Zeland, Vadim. *Reality Transurfing. Steps I-V.* CreateSpace Independent Publishing Platform, 2016. Kindle.

Printed in Great Britain
by Amazon